Tips for Christian Singles

Love
Hangover

Moving from
Pain to Purpose
After a Relationship Ends

"*Shewanda Riley's* **Love Hangover** *is a salve on the wounds of the broken-hearted. This is a vital word of healing and hope for those in pain. She offers godly counsel in the face of broken promises and dreams, leading the reader to learn as she did, that God is working for the best in the midst of it all. I recommend this book for all. It is great preventive medicine as well.*"

—*Dr. Sheron C. Patterson*
Senior Pastor, St. Paul United Methodist Church, Dallas,
Founder and author (The Love Clinic)

"**Love Hangover** *offers readers life-changing insight into how to successfully heal from one of the most common yet painful of human conditions—the broken heart. Riley and Hawkins provide a vivid and memorable testimony of the power of God to transform. This is a must read that will change how singles see themselves and relationships.*"

—*Les Brown*
Motivational Speaker and international best-selling author
(It's Not Over Until You Win)

"*This is a unique and well-written book that provides valuable insight and practical examples on how to rely on God and rebuild your emotional and spiritual strength when weakened by a broken heart and broken relationship. I highly recommend it to both men and women!*"

—*Edward C. Nicholson, Ph.D.*
Commissioner, United Professional Football League

Tips for Christian Singles

Love
Hangover

Moving from
Pain to Purpose
After a Relationship Ends

Shewanda Riley with
Germaine Hawkins, Ph.D.

SunCreek
B O O K S
Allen, Texas

Acknowledgments:

All scripture quotations, unless otherwise indicated, are taken from the New
King James Version. Copyright © 1982 by Thomas Nelson, Inc. Used by
permission. All rights reserved.

Scripture quotations marked (NIV) are taken from the HOLY BIBLE, NEW
INTERNATIONAL VERSION®. NIV®. Copyright © 1973, 1978, 1984 by
International Bible Society. Used by permission of Zondervan. All rights
reserved.

Send all inquiries to:
SunCreek Books
An RCL Company
200 East Bethany Drive
Allen, Texas 75002-3804

Telephone: 800-264-0368 / 972-390-6300
Fax: 800-688-8356 / 972-390-6560

Visit us at: **www.thomasmore.com**
Customer Service E-mail: **cservice@rcl-enterprises.com**

Printed in the United States of America

Library of Congress Control Number: 2002102198

5701   ISBN 1-932057-01-3

1 2 3 4 5   06 05 04 03 02

"If you are single and in love—or ever hope to be—this a great book that won't prevent your heart from being broken, but will surely help to mend it if it does."

—Stephen Arterburn
Founder, Women of Faith, and host, New Life Live!
Author, Avoiding Mr. Wrong

"If you've ever been hurt or disappointed in a love relationship and found it hard to live with yourself and forgive them, this is the book for you. It's authentic, practical, God inspired wisdom will empower you with the confidence and commitment to live happily ever after a Love Hangover."

—Thelma Wells
President, Woman of God Ministries, Mother of Zion Ministries
Speaker, Women of Faith Conference

"Finally, a book that honestly covers an area that men and women often take too lightly . . . the life-changing impact of a broken heart and the shattered dreams that follow. I enthusiastically recommend it to anyone who wants to know how to fix a broken heart!"

—Honorable Leo V. Chaney, Jr., J.D.
Dallas City Council, District 7

"Riley and Hawkins deliver potent truth with this straightforward prescription for a love hangover. After reading this, we should all be cured!"

—William July
Author (Brothers, Lust and Love *and* Understanding The Tin Man)

To the memory of
my greatgrandmother Pearlie B. Matthews
and my grandfather Frank Riley, Sr.
—Shewanda Riley

To the memory of my father,
Robert Lee Hawkins (1939–1996)
—Germaine Hawkins

Contents

Introduction 9

Part 1 Courage 17

Chapter 1   The Mirror Doesn't Lie: Playing the Blame Game 19

Chapter 2   Truth—The Thorny Beauty 27

Chapter 3   Half-Empty or Half-Full 35

Whispers of Love—Pause for Reflection 46

Part 2 Affirmation 49

Chapter 4   Living and Loving in Moderation 51

Chapter 5   Treasures of the Heart 59

Chapter 6   Is That Your final Answer? 65

Whispers of Love—Pause for Reflection 72

Part 3 Confidence 75

Chapter 7   Betrayal by Any Other Name 77

Chapter 8   Letting Go Gracefully 91

Chapter 9   Thinking Outside the Box 99

Whispers of Love—Pause for Reflection 104

Part 4 Love **107**

Chapter 10   Is It Love . . . or Are You a Bellywarmer? 109

Chapter 11   Sister to Brother . . . Brother to Sister 121

Whispers of Love—Pause for Reflection 133

Part 5 Joy **137**

Chapter 12   Breaking Soul Ties 139

Chapter 13   Toxic People and How to Avoid Them! 151

Whispers of Love—Pause for Reflection 168

Part 6 Affirmation **171**

Chapter 14   How Does Your Garden Grow? 173

Chapter 15   A View from the Other Side 189

Whispers of Love—Pause for Reflection 201

Appendix A   When All Else Fails . . . See the Doctor 205

Appendix B   Recommended Websites 215

Recommended Books 216

Scripture Index 219

Author Biographies and Acknowledgements 221

Introduction

GOD, THIS IS *NOT* WHAT I PRAYED FOR! In fact, you must not have heard my prayer or you misunderstood. Remember, I prayed for you to show me my boyfriend's intentions and plans concerning our relationship. After all, we've dated for nearly one and a half years. I prayed for you to show me where his heart was concerning our relationship. Him ending the relationship was not, I repeat, *NOT* what I asked for!

In November 1999, I was looking at my sad, tear-streaked face in the mirror and repeating those words. Though I really didn't like the answer, God, as always, was faithful and *had* answered my prayer. However, being dumped by my boyfriend with the explanation "God told me to do this" was not exactly what I'd expected. I expected him to ask me to marry him. We'd been dating long enough and he'd stated repeatedly to me and to others who asked that that's what we were working toward. We had even been featured guests on radio shows and at singles workshops talking about our relationship.

I remember being so disappointed after accepting the hard reality that God's answer to my prayer did not match my hopes of having a future with my boyfriend. I still remember my boyfriend's answer one month before our breakup when someone at the church where he was a minister asked when we were getting married. His very confident, public statement was as it had been for so long: "We're working on it." Apparently the "we" was not the two of us: he married an ex-girlfriend eight months later. The most bitter pill to swallow was the fact that although I was very serious about spending the rest of my life with him, he was not at all serious about spending his with me.

For the first few months after the breakup, I was so numb all I did was either cry or mutter over and over (and sometimes at the same time), "I can't believe this is happening! I just can't believe it!" I became concerned after three months when my feelings for my ex hadn't changed. Even after being told by him that nothing other than our *first* date should have happened, I still loved him and was in love with him! Like a fool, I still wanted to see him and talk to him. A few times I gathered the courage to call him, but was always disappointed with the stilted conversation and obvious disinterest in his voice. It didn't make sense and, in fact, it was crazy. He left me but I still wanted him! My feelings were out of control; it was like I was drunk and out of my right mind. It was like having a hangover—all the joy of the experience was gone. All that was left was a headache from crying too much, a stomachache from not eating, and a heartache from losing my love. Unlike Diana Ross, who proclaimed in her 1977 disco anthem "Love Hangover" that "if there's a cure for this, I don't want it . . . don't need it," I did.

Scientists define a hangover as the body's reaction to an excess of toxins in the system. Because these toxins are in the blood, it takes time for the body to naturally cleanse itself. Similarly, once a relationship ends, it takes time for "toxins," like the burden of shame, the irrationality of anger, and the sting of rejection, to leave your emotional system. I define a love hangover as emotions, thoughts, feelings, and attitudes that remain from what is past, which often includes the disappointment following the end of a relationship. For me, it took years of prayer, fasting, counseling, and seeking the Lord to cleanse my system and cure me of my "love hangover."

By reading about my process of recovery, I hope you will realize that emotional healing is possible and that, even after a disappointing heartbreak, you can love again and be loved. I have included entries from a journal I kept during my love hangover. I pray that these entries will help you realize, like I did, that the key to recovering from your love hangover is to accept that it is not about what the ex did to you, but *your* reaction to the breakup. You must become emotionally responsible and allow God to change how you feel about yourself and about the relationship.

> **RECOVERY TIP:**
> *The key to recovering from a love hangover is to accept that it's not about what your ex did— it's about you becoming emotionally responsible.*

In other words, the love hangover is not about rebuilding your relationship with your ex, it's about rebuilding your relationship with God. My purpose in writing this book is not to expose my ex-boyfriend; it is to expose me. It is not to cast judgment on him or me for what went wrong; it is merely to provide a road map of recovery. Like all maps, it can be used every step of the way or just for certain parts of the journey. My hope is that others will be healed from destructive relationships and the debilitating effects of unhealthy relationships.

For those of you who are wondering what this has to do with a hangover and when we are going to get to the "good stuff" (you know, the fights that happened in the relationship), a special note: This book is about what happened to me after the relationship ended. In working through my love hangover, I realized that after the relationship ends, it doesn't matter who did what to whom and why. It's not even that important that you reconcile your relationship with that person, but that you restore your relationship with God. The most painful truth about the love hangover is that it shows that there is a problem, not with your ex, but with your relationship with God. As you read this book and journey toward wholeness, know that God is with you.

What causes a love hangover? And what in the past contributes to the seering and seemingly never-ending pain? Toxins in the system. Low self-esteem, unresolved anger, codependent relationships are some examples that quickly come to mind. For me, it was the idea that I couldn't keep a man. I've loved a lot of men, but have only been in love with three: my ex-boyfriend in Miami, my ex-husband, and my most recent ex-boyfriend. All three of these men were "taken away" by other women, with two of them ending in marriage. The relationships ending this way did such damage to my already low self-esteem. I was left wondering: What is it that these women have that I don't, that they can keep a man, but I can't? I can flirt and get them in relationship, but I can't keep them! I compared myself to my own sisters, who'd had boyfriends and husbands clamoring for their love and attention when I couldn't buy a date. I even went through a period where I didn't have a date for almost two years.

I remember sharing this fear with my most recent ex-boyfriend with the hope that he would understand my concerns about what I felt was his inappropriately close relationship with the woman who is now, coincidently, his wife. I thought that by sharing those concerns, I would be able to face the fear head-on and eventually overcome the grip it had had on my life. I know now that part of this fear was rooted in my own unfounded childhood thoughts of not being good enough for my father's love. As an adult, I can see that both my parents loved me and my three sisters, in different ways but with equal amounts of care and sensitivity.

Despite my love for the Lord and the cry of my heart to be healed and to know him better, I was unable to focus on the scripture that clearly defines what love is 1 Corinthians 13:4–8. I couldn't see God's love in the suffering that I was experiencing. Nor did I want to be patient or kind. I was still too hurt. And all I could do at some points was

> **RECOVERY TIP:**
> *Ask God to show you yourself.*
> *It takes courage to change your prayer from "God, why did he do this?" to "God, show me, me!"*

to think evil. It was through the process of recovery and healing that I began to see that this scripture showed how little godly love existed in my relationship with my ex. God's arms of protection and love holding me during this time showed that this passage of scripture held the keys to my opening up the door for true emotional healing. I got lost at times and distracted by the opinions of others and I lost sight of the fact that God wanted to heal me as much as I wanted to be healed. This scripture and others provided the compass I needed for my road to recovery and restoration.

Tormented once again with thoughts of my being less of a woman because I couldn't keep a man, I realized that I had to deal with this issue. To be healthy and enjoy a healthy relationship, I would have to understand why I felt this way. I would have to turn the spotlight off my ex and back onto myself. My prayer then changed from "God, show me why he did this to me" to "God, show me, me!"

Rather than focus on the "why," courageously ask God to show you what he wants you to learn (not that the other person just wasn't the one or why *they* were wrong.) Ask God to show you "yourself" and his heart concerning you. Be prepared for the answer, but patient and obedient enough to be still and wait on God. It may seem like God is not hearing you or is confused because he has not shown you what you want. Remember that God knows what he is doing.

What else can you do to start your recovery process? During this time other wounded hearts and spirits will be strangely attracted to you. Like attracts like. You'll have a wonderful pity party but still feel the same afterward. Try to not surround yourself with people who provide what sounds and feels good temporarily, but offers no true emotional or spiritual healing.

What are some things that you can do when you decide to get over your love hangover? Pray for God to surround you with people, friends, and wise counselors who will provide an emotional anchor during this time. One rule to keep in mind: It's the quality, not the quantity, of friends that will be critical to uplift you, especially when you can't pray for yourself.

This book is a written road map of my journey to recovery. Like any road map, it can be used for none, some, or all of the journey. It's there when you need it most at any particular point in your journey to recovery. Because it's easiest to express myself in writing, during my recovery period I journaled. Sometimes I wrote as little as once a day, sometimes more than three times, depending on my emotional state. Because I had no contact with my ex and very little contact with others, my journal became my best friend, one that I looked forward to communing with at my most difficult emotional times.

Written during the darkest times in my heartbreak, my entries are full of raw, sincere emotions. I hope that by sharing these thoughts and feelings with you, you'll see that recovery is possible and that you are not alone. Each chapter of this book includes explanations of the journal entries and a "post-hangover" reflection. The post-hangover reflections reveal what I learned most about myself at each point in the recovery.

This book will only show one version of the recovery process. Recovery often involves counselors, ministers, and therapy encouraging the patient to "get over it." But once I understood it the way I felt God intended, I realized that the process of recovery is much more intimate; there are no time limits or constraints.

The recovery process begins as we focus on ourselves and ends as we shift our focus to our position within our community of faith. Our path of emotional recovery continues at church, with the loving support and care of other believers. It is in this community that we are protected by a safe haven to develop healthy relationships.

Part I

COURAGE

*Cause me to hear
your lovingkindness
in the morning,
For in You do I trust;
Cause me to know the way
in which I should walk,
For I lift up my soul to You.*

Psalm 143:8

"COURAGE IS ONE STEP AHEAD OF FEAR."

—Coleman Young

An individual's inner strength is a critical element in the recipe for success in any endeavor. The pain and disappointment that are part of the package deal in matters of the heart can sometimes create an inner battle. Am I weak, or am I strong? The heart will wonder, even in the midst of trying, "Can I really do this?" and your actions must demonstrate an answer that says, "Yes." Reflections on past mistakes can cause you to question, "If I'm supposed to be so strong, how did I get into this mess?" It is not that you are inherently weak, but that you were walking in weakness at that time. Deciding to be strong—to utilize the reserves of courage inside the core of your personhood—can be the catalyst to changing your recovery experience from one surrounded by a fear of failure to one assured of success.

> *"You are of God, little children,*
> *and have overcome them,*
> *because He who is in you is greater*
> *than he who is in the world."*
>
> 1 John 4:4

Chapter 1

The Mirror Doesn't Lie—
Stop Playing the Blame Game

I thirst right now for peace of mind. I'm so hurt, angry, frustrated and confused. I hate him and everything that he stands for. My desire is to be whole. I want to understand why I feel such a void, why I feel so empty. I need you so much now, God . . . and I'm scared.

THIS JOURNAL ENTRY was written two days after my boyfriend announced that "God" had told him we needed to take a two-month break. After pleading for more specific details of why and how and what was going on, I decided to give him his space and to use that time for God to "grow me up."

It was a painful decision and I cried as I walked out of his apartment; I cried as I sat in my car trying to get it started; and I cried as I drove home. In fact, I think I set a new record for the amount of tears shed in a week. I didn't know that I had that many tears inside of me. My family was hundreds of miles away, and for the year and a half that we'd dated, my boyfriend was my best friend, so I had no one else to whom I could turn.

What hurt so much was that he now acted as if he had never loved me. In fact, he told me that other than our first date, which we both agreed God had orchestrated, nothing in our relationship should have happened. Wow! That really hurt me. He was an ordained minister and pastor, and he told me I had hindered his ministry. But even after hearing these painful words, I still loved him. I still wanted to be with him. I still wanted him. I felt like I was crazy to even want a man who told me, "I know I devastated you," without so much as an apology or explanation.

I have inner clutter that is the pain and brokenness from childhood and past relationships. My fear of abandonment and then the anger that occurs when it happens. I can feel that there is a void and am seeking to fill it. Is this right . . . anger and fear and low self-esteem and feeling like I am unable to do anything about it?

I WROTE THIS ENTRY just a few weeks after the breakup. I realized that there was something very wrong with me. Instead of being able to quickly shake off the feelings of loss, I was having a hard time functioning in my day-to-day activities. I went to my daytime radio job and worked as a part-time college professor at night, but I wasn't doing very well at either job. I'd been unemployed for five months and had prayed for those jobs specifically, yet I wasn't able to even thank God for those blessings because I was distracted by my emotional pain.

More than anything, confusion began to take over and I felt abandoned by God. In the midst of this great emotional and spiritual crisis, I wanted to be and feel spiritually and emotionally healthy, and this became my focus.

A friend once told me about his experience with an alcoholic hangover. He proudly described not remembering what he ate, how he got up the stairs to bed, and how he woke up the next morning still in his clothes. His description of the events leading up to the hangover and his perception of this night of fun reminded me of my perceptions of the circumstances leading to my own "love hangover."

> 🌼 RECOVERY TIP: *Avoid exaggerating the positive or negative aspects of the relationship— magnifying the memories will only prolong the love hangover.*

It wasn't until he was clear-headed the next morning that he could enjoy the memories of the experience which far outshone the realities of the experience. Sometimes we compensate for the foolish things we have done by minimizing the experience and magnifying the memory. Consider failed relationships. I've had to honestly ask myself how often this coping skill has allowed me to regain the control over my emotions that I had lost or assumed I had lost as a result of my love hangover.

Through the Lord's mercies we are not consumed,
Because His compassions fail not. They are new every morning;
Great is Your faithfulness. Lamentations 3:22–23

After the smoke clears, the harsh and bitter words spoken and the tears dried, you're now faced with both the *morning* and the *mourning* after. If you are like many who have gone through a difficult breakup, you minimize the power the relationship had over your life and your emotions and you say things like, "I didn't really like him . . . but I sure liked his money. I was the one running him;" or "I never really loved her but I sure did like the sex we had." I did this same thing by magnifying the negative part of the relationship while I remained unwilling to admit that there was something about my ex that I valued and that I benefited from the relationship. Otherwise, I wouldn't have wasted my time.

It was hard, but I had to avoid exaggerating the positive or negative details of the relationship. At times it was difficult to accept that the relationship had ended. I eventually realized that it was unhealthy and dangerous to prolong my "love hangover" by trying to control the memories. I had to work hard at not allowing my feelings of powerlessness during the hangover to turn into the natural response of overcontrol in the other areas of my life.

But I will sing of Your power; Yes, I will sing aloud
of Your mercy in the morning; For you have been my defense
And refuge in the day of my trouble. Psalm 59:16

I am a morning person, and I get more done before 11:00 A.M. than any other time of the day. I look forward to getting a fresh start on the day and getting things done in the morning, so I can enjoy the afternoon and evening. I can appreciate the morning now after my relationship ended and God has changed me dramatically. Now that my head has cleared and I can see what emotional toxins were in my system, I can't believe that I did and said "those" things. I can't believe I let "those" things be done to me. As I went through the mourning of my relationship, I also learned to appreciate this time, because I slowly let go of the need to control and relaxed enough to enjoy the comfort of God being in control.

It is after my therapy session and I feel very raw and vulnerable. My counselor stated some very true and painful things ... that I was a controller, that I was afraid, and that I needed restoration. She also stated that if I truly believed in the relationship, I needed to contact my ex and share with him some of the things from our session. I'm so scared, I don't know if I can do it. I must recognize that this is an unhealthy and destructive pattern of relationship. I must trust in God's promises and stop trying to control the situation and trying to be God. My counselor also stated that I needed to see that my ex loved me the best way he could and that I loved him the best way I could.

> **RECOVERY TIP:**
> *Apologize to your ex for what you understand to be your part in the breakup of the relationship—it will help you move toward emotional wholeness.*

P RIOR TO OUR BREAKUP, I started counseling sessions twice a month with a pastoral care counselor to help me as I struggled through an unusually long period of unemployment and underemployment. Ironically, she also encouraged me to shift my focus from external circumstances and to look deeper into changes I needed to make internally. The above entry was written after a very open session and shows my reaction to what I believed were harsh words from her.

I admit that I was very angry at her after the session. I told her during the session that she really couldn't see how much was his fault. At one point, she stopped me and told me that her issue was not blaming him and neither should it be mine. I thought she was crazy to suggest that I meet with him and apologize. After all, he was the one who hurt me. I thought that if anyone needed to apologize, it was him. I resented her telling me to do something that would add to the humiliation that I was already feeling. It was only after I did apologize that I realized that she was merely trying to free me from my prison of anger with the key of forgiveness.

There are times when cussing and crying are all that I feel like doing. How do I overcome all of these hard experiences and not repeat the same mistakes?

Taking the advice of my counselor, today I met with my ex and I told him some very heartfelt feelings about our relationship. I was so nervous but I felt better telling him that I couldn't offer him the kind of friendship he was looking for. I wanted to make sure that what I was saying was about how I felt and not trying to hurt or manipulate him. I now finally feel that I can start moving on with my life. I miss him and God, you know how much I love him . . . but right now I love myself more.

What was so liberating about our meeting? Maybe because I apologized for trying to control him. I apologized for trying to get in the way of his relationships with others. I apologized for my emotional instability during my recent and ongoing time of unemployment.

I told him that I needed space but that I was sure that eventually we could probably be friends like he wanted. He said that he worried about me and prayed for me every day. . . . Big deal! I don't think he really understands how serious a breach of trust this is for me.

I FELT SO LIBERATED after I met with my ex. Even though I accepted responsibility for my part in the relationship, by apologizing I was reducing the possibility of the blame game being played. Because I was able to honestly express what I felt, I was slowly moving toward emotional wholeness. I was slowly moving toward the point where it didn't matter to me whether I saw him or not. My focus was on becoming stronger emotionally and spiritually.

Truthfully, I still didn't agree with his decision, but I loved him enough to let him go. I could have begged and pleaded for another chance, but I respected myself too much to beg him to love me. Even though I felt a tinge of stupidity for apologizing, the overwhelming sense of freedom made even those feelings quickly disappear.

> **RECOVERY TIP:**
> *Change your traveling companions from fear and blame to courage and responsibility—it's the only way to get through a love hangover.*

I feared meeting face to face the man who'd forced me to leave broken dreams and unfulfilled promises behind. I just didn't think I was ready to do that. It was a hard lesson, but I learned that the only way I could make it through was to change my traveling companions from fear and blame to courage and responsibility.

Post-Love Hangover Reflection

IN THE REBUILDING PROCESS, I had to accept that there may actually be *no one* to blame! Being able to accept this relieved some of the stress caused by the uncertainty of my relationship breakup.

I am amazed at the depth and crippling effect of my pain. These seemingly baby steps were the hardest to take . . . not because I didn't want to distance myself from the relationship, but because I was afraid of what I was leaving behind.

Having the answer or at least a partial answer became somewhat therapeutic, but I had to accept that it is also okay to not have an answer to some things.

Imagine the mindset of an architect or a civil engineer. He envisions elaborate and intricate works that will one day house or even entertain thousands of people. However, he stands alone on Mother Earth. His desire and his faith together comprise his power drill. His tools? Steel. Iron. Lumber. Glass. Sheetrock. With these basic things he *believes* he can build something of greatness to be revered, respected, valued, and admired by many. I had to have this same confidence as I made the decision to courageously walk out of brokenness and into a life of spiritual and emotional wholeness.

Chapter 2

Truth—
The Thorny Beauty

I just got an e-mail from my ex-boyfriend, you know, one of those you send to all fifty of your e-mail buddies. In the e-mail, he gave his new e-mail address. My question is this: why would he give me his new e-mail address and website information? Does he not understand that this is not the space I was asking for? What's wrong with him?

I thank you, God, for loving me enough to show me where I need to improve. It's a very painfully revealing time for me. I pray I can make it through. I hope I don't get halfway through it and turn back out of fear. I realize that my stains are anger, fear of rejection, and abandonment. Lord, help me to wash the stains from this painful experience from my life. I am slowly realizing the purpose of this lesson is to help myself and others.

   I pray that my view of you, God, is not that you are a God who demands sacrifice . . . keep reminding me that free will is what you honor.

Rereading my journals, I realize that I'm doing okay. I'm still hurt but the anger and pain are subsiding. After having

> *Thanksgiving weekend to reflect, I realize that I don't even*
> *want to deal with a friendship from him. This means that no*
> *phone calls from him and no visits will be a very good thing.*
> *I decided this because when I saw him the day before*
> *Thanksgiving, he was still interested in knowing what I was*
> *going to do for Thanksgiving. I told him that I was going out*
> *of town. I asked him if he still loved me. Very emphatically he*
> *stated that he still did and would always love me. Kind of*
> *strange. I don't know if I believed him, but it was nice to*
> *hear, even if it was a lie.*

I WROTE THESE ENTRIES within the same week and they exhibit the emotional roller coaster I was on. I was thankful to God for showing me that my ex didn't love me as much as I loved him, yet I was still angry that my ex professed to others that we were still friends. He made the choice for the breakup to be nasty; if it had been up to me, we still would have been friends. I didn't understand why he would e-mail me. At this point in the breakup I really began to hunger for a clearer truth about myself, my ex, and the relationship.

Interestingly, the Lord also allowed me to see my ex's peculiar reaction to the breakup. He called a few times and shared with me details of his life (trips, job promotion), but grew cold in the conversations when I wanted to talk about how he felt about the current state of our relationship. Granted, it took me a few times to realize that it was a game, and I soon decided I didn't want to play. Once this happened, I stopped returning his calls.

Because I desired more wisdom and insight from God, I had to increase my time of intimate fellowship with him. I began to pray more and asked God to increase my confidence in knowing that my prayers would be answered. I wasn't praying for reconciliation; I was praying for greater clarity from God on the situation. Truth, no matter how painful, was more important than anything at this point.

I was still struggling and boldly trying to face and deal with truth. It was difficult to hold on because I didn't have the adequate tools. I was seeing my counselor and making progress, but it was hard to deal with the potency of the truth. It was overwhelming. I was beginning to focus more on my life and concentrate less on the possibilities of restoring the relationship.

As is obvious from the journals, I also was still fighting God on fully accepting the changes that were occurring in my life. Obedience was an issue for me, but it was clear that I would have to do something about it. I was trying to handle it by controlling my emotions, but God wanted me to just surrender.

In my search for greater intimacy with God, I recognized the importance of fasting and consecration. I wasn't using it as a quick fix for my problems, but I knew from past experiences that I would become more intimate with God if I submitted myself in obedience. When I was dating my ex I did not maintain my time of consecration through fasting and prayer. I recall at some point in my relationship feeling remorse because I'd stopped fasting. I went back to fasting from food all day at least once a week and I immediately noticed a difference in my intimacy with God. My situation hadn't changed, but I was able to better accept the truth. No longer seeing truth as something to hurt others with, like my ex had hurt me, I began seeing it as something good. But truth sometimes has to be handled delicately to avoid hurting others. Truth is like rose petals that open and close in due time, come in different shades like red and yellow, share the plant with thorns that force you to handle it carefully, and add a sweet fragrance and aroma.

I had to accept the reality of my ex's character after I looked at myself. I realized that if I focused on him and then on myself that I could end up in a vicious cycle of shame and blame. Forcing myself to deal with "me" made it easier to deal with him. I had to have compassion to deal mercifully and gracefully with his faults as God had compassion to deal with mine. Without doing so, I ran the risk of being judgmental.

> **RECOVERY TIP:**
> *Handle the truth delicately, like handling a rose. It's something good that comes in many shapes and many varieties—it's not meant to hurt, but it can.*

Remember, it is only after you've allowed God's grace to change you that you can then encourage the same thing in others. But it is equally important that you honestly assess the other person's role and responsibility in the relationship.

I had a conversation with a friend who said that he found freedom from the bondage of a past relationship when he told his ex-wife that she was wrong. He didn't tell her out of anger but out of a realization that she had taken advantage of him, used his kids, and manipulated him. As long as he was in denial about her true character, he remained vulnerable to allowing her to continue playing games with him. He stated that it was so liberating to tell her.

Acknowledging your true character and wrongdoing as well as your former partner's, will bring a balanced sense of closure to the relationship because it forces you to look at both sides. It is so much easier to look only at yourself (shaming) or at your ex (blaming). God wants us as Christians to lead balanced, victorious lives and to accept responsibility for ourselves.

"You can't handle the truth!" was shouted at a general during the infamous courtroom scene of the military court drama *A Few Good Men*. I thought during this time that I couldn't handle the truth. What I didn't realize was that I was actually trying to handle my own desire to accept falsehoods disguised as truth.

When I examined my ex's true character, I realized it was foolish to say, "He was a good man." "Good" men don't abandon their responsibilities and run from difficult situations and relationships. "Good" women don't cheat and lie. "Good" people don't expose your worst fears and insecurities to others in order to make themselves look better. Stop fooling yourself and see what God is showing you. Stop lying to yourself and to other people about who you and your ex are. If you have character problems, acknowledge it. That's the only way God can truly start the relationship and emotional healing process.

> **RECOVERY TIP:**
> *Avoid the shame and blame syndromes—assess both sides of the relationship and acknowledge your true character and wrongdoing, as well as that of your former partner.*

During my recovery time I read *Avoiding Mr. Wrong* by Stephen Arterburn and Meg Rinck (Thomas Nelson, 2000). The book describes ten kinds of men who cause havoc in the lives of women through destructive and manipulative ways. I was so shocked when I saw my ex in all ten. This chilling realization forced me to see that he didn't have my best interests at heart; he did not cherish me and he did not value our friendship. He proved this by cutting off communication and saying hurtful things. Regretfully, I imagined that there was something wrong with me and that's why he didn't care.

I realized after reading the book, that my ex's inability to cherish me was his problem—not mine. If I chose to make it mine, it would keep me in bondage and free him from accepting his emotional responsibility. You should feel free to remember both the good and the bad. I had to say that the relationship was important to me; doing the opposite would keep me in bondage to the deceptive hope that the relationship was good. The relationship was an important part of my life—he and his family were important to me. To minimize everything we had formed while dating or casually dismiss the dating relationship as a mistake (as he had) put myself in the position of being God to judge purposes. I believe that all people come into my life for a reason; the season we were intimate was just as important as the season of absence that followed.

Amazingly, it was very difficult to accept that he had a hand in our breakup. Even though he initiated it, I was sadly willing to accept full responsibility for the relationship not working. I felt so worthless and meaningless that it was easier to accept complete blame.

Because I was still in emotional bondage and traumatized by the breakup, I refused to accept the promised freedom of the truth of his responsibilities. After all, someone had to take responsibility for the end; since he'd walked away, I felt like I had to be the one.

My ex's statement, "Other than our first date, nothing should have happened," wreaked havoc on my emotional state. Were we wrong to date? Considering the way it ended, maybe he was right and I was wrong. . . . I'd been wrong before with my ex-husband. I constantly questioned my judgment and decision-making ability.

Not until I thought about other relationships that developed as a result of our dating was I able to convince myself that we both had benefited from the relationship. Otherwise, it wouldn't have lasted so long. By accepting his version, I was robbing myself of my memories of the relationship. I had to search for and establish a balanced truth. The balanced truth recognizes the good and bad parts about ourselves, about our partners, and about our relationships.

Post-Love Hangover Reflection

As CRAZY AS IT SOUNDS, I'm glad that I had this particular struggle. It has humbled me and made me realize that I didn't have it all "together." Consequently, my recovery was tailor-made by God just for me. Advice from others helped at some point. However, the most important factor in growing emotionally stronger and spiritually wiser has been my willingness to obey and submit to God. What I thought was obedience was in some cases blind, immature faith. As hard as it was to accept, I now realize that recognizing the truth is only the first step to recovery. Willful submission is the next step of growth.

> RECOVERY TIP:
> *Seek the balanced truth. Do not accept sole responsibility for the breakup of the relationship—it will only cause emotional bondage and trauma.*

Chapter 3

Half-Empty or Half-Full—
The Choice Is Yours

I realize that I cling to and clutch onto old ideas and beliefs about myself, such as I am not good enough or someone else is more important than me. Right now the notion that I don't have what it takes to keep a man, or keep him happy, is so very painful. These protect me from my vulnerabilities and from facing my fears. I'm afraid to be alone. I don't want to live by myself. I want close friends who support me. I strangely push away those who could seemingly help me the most. I want to give up control, but don't know how. Please God, show me how.

I can see so much growth in my journals. I feel stronger than last week though the pain weakens me sometimes. I am making great progress. Thank you, God, for staying with me and loving me and also for loving him. I recently saw someone who had some interesting things to say about our breakup. She'd seen him recently and said that he acted like it didn't bother him that we'd broken up. She also said that he told her that our breakup was a mutual decision. I told her that he initiated the breakup. When she asked me if I spoke to his mother about it I told her that I had nothing to do with him or his family. She seemed surprised but I could tell she was fishing for information. Why would he misrepresent the truth like that? Is it because he ultimately cannot bear the responsibility? How scary for a pastor to be! This makes me sad and mad—sad because it's another sign of his immaturity and mad because it is a lie.

Rereading my journals, I am pleasantly surprised by the inch-by-inch growth in my emotions. I still have moments when I am angry and experience seering pain. I am thankful that even during these times, that I know that you, God, are still gingerly and tenderly holding me. But I am still very lonesome sometimes.

OVER A TWO-WEEK PERIOD about six weeks after the breakup, I challenged myself to change my perspective. I was waffling between trying to understand and accept my heartbreak. I was having the hardest time because I wanted to understand something that God merely wanted me to accept. My desire to understand was keeping me from peacefully accepting the end of the relationship.

Because I couldn't grasp what was going on mentally, emotionally and spiritually, I saw my life as a mess. I was working hard to find the elements in my life that confirmed that. I was just finishing my first semester as an adjunct English professor at a community college and was still transitioning into my new job as news director for a Dallas radio station. Every little thing that went wrong I blamed on my being such a loser. I thought that my being such a loser in love was also translating into my employment.

Even though I was now doing professionally what I'd always wanted to do, I somehow couldn't see it as a blessing. And one reason is because I didn't feel worthy of the blessings. In my mind, if I was really worthy, I could have held onto my ex. This was a result of the confusion from the conflict to understand and accept. I was trying to understand how God could bless me when he just wanted me to accept the blessings.

> RECOVERY TIP:
> *Think about the big picture—it's not just your life and his life. If your relationship wasn't positively impacting others, maybe it wasn't so good after all.*

It finally dawned on me that God was rebuilding and restoring me, but I only saw that when I changed my perspective on the way things were going. I couldn't understand why this was an area of such great struggle. More than anything, it gave me an honest picture of what I thought about myself, which greatly influenced how others saw me too.

I reached a milestone when I stopped compartmentalizing and started looking at the bigger picture. It wasn't just about my "life" and his "life"; it was about how we positively impacted others. We'd shown so many others through our appearances on radio shows and singles ministry programs that you could have a successful relationship and be a Christian Single. He commented often that he somewhat enjoyed being the featured couple. This was after we did a singles program for the Potter's House Singles Ministry. If our relationship wasn't doing that, maybe it wasn't such a good relationship after all.

My emotional focus was now on the yearnings I felt. Now that I'd been exposed to and forced to accept the truth that our relationship wasn't a healthy or holy one, it was doubtful to me whether God was even pleased with it. Now I had to do something with that truth.

I hate to admit it, but I'm still looking for the blessing in this "thing" that has happened with my ex. I still don't understand nor am I able to let go of the pain. I don't want to be bitter. I want to be whole. I want to know the blessing; please show me the blessing. Is this why I must not give up so I can see the blessing in the ruins of the relationship? Please, God, help me. I don't like feeling this way.

Something for which I am grateful but rarely give thanks is the ability to keep trying. I have a fighter's spirit and winner's mentality (most of the time). I keep trying and the tenacity often is what is the blessing. So I can see that rather than give up on hopeless situations (much like my five-month job search), I must maintain that same level of faith and trust in you, God. This year has been a year of holding onto your promises (that is a difficult thing). My prayer is that I'll continue to be able to remain balanced and spiritually sound.

It's the day after Christmas and I'm very hurt because he did not call. I am so disappointed and disgusted because the least he could have done was call to wish me a Merry Christmas. He did it for his ex last year—what am I, chopped liver? Anyway, I cried through the night and while preparing for church, I had a meltdown. Why even after two months am I still grieving? Why can't I move on? I've been meditating on certain Scriptures, like Philippians 4:8, but they don't seem to be working. I feel like such a loser! Is what I did and said so wrong that I deserve this? Why, God, has this happened?

Please, dear God, don't leave me here! I've never not gone to church because of this type of stuff. I've got to get stronger. Please, dear God, don't leave me. What am I supposed to do?

> **RECOVERY TIP:**
> *Accept the fact that the holidays will be painful after a breakup—pray for strength and endurance, and lean on some of your friends for support.*

After my meltdown, I called my counselor and she told me very firmly that I needed to move on with my life—that's what he'd done. I told her that even though I'd told him not to call me, I at least expected a brief call on Christmas—I mean, it's Christmas and he knows that I'm away from my family. After hanging up with her, I decided that I needed to know the truth. My prayer is that I would know the truth—but about what? Not sure; or maybe I'm afraid to ask about what. I decided to call him and pitch the idea of us reconciling our friendship. This thought had been in my heart for at least a week, but I fought it. I prayed about it and realized that God did not want us as Christians to be at odds and that he wanted us reconciled. I hope I have the courage to do it. I paged him around 2:30 P.M. because I knew that he would be out of church and on his way to his mother's house.

After speaking with him a few hours ago, I am now at peace but also disturbed. At peace, because the truth of the situation is that he is making some awful excuses about why he has not called. (1) He was mad and (2) I told him not to. Now that he says he is no longer mad, I told him that I felt it was okay for him to call. Let's see what happens. I have a feeling that there is another reason why he is not calling— could it be another woman (that would actually make more sense than his stated reasons)? He is not being honest, but what else is new? However, I'm not going to spend the rest of my life trying to figure out why.

When I told him that I thought as Christians we should reconcile our friendship, he stated very coldly that he still considered me a friend, but that I was one of his friends that he just never called. He added that we obviously have different views of friendship. At that point, I had to agree with him.

One thing I did ask him is if he still believed as he'd told me earlier that I hindered his ministry and that he lost his focus (on what, I don't know) while we were dating, why would he want to be my friend. He didn't have a response to that.

The last thing I told him was that if he ever needed to talk about anything, he could feel free to call me. His response: yeah sure. I don't think he'll call, but at least I offered. That hurt because I really wanted him to know that I was not trying to trick him back into a relationship with me (and told him so), but just believed that God wanted our friendship reconciled. I was very nervous, but I did get the words out of my mouth. Then I cried myself to sleep.

THE BREAKUP LEFT ME with a lot of quiet time. I don't think I've ever spent so much time in prayer. I was working two jobs and had to work hard to find the time when I wasn't preoccupied with work and work-related issues. The best time for me ended up being at the end of my day, right before I fell asleep. This is the time I spent my last hour of consciousness talking to God and also writing in my journal. I watched very little if any television and talked on the telephone only when required. My pain had driven me to becoming a hermit and somewhat antisocial. I think I needed the solitude to really hear God and get my emotions back on track with his will. I don't recommend it lasting for more than a few months. At that point, it's no longer protection; it's an excuse for building a wall of exclusion. Remember, when you build a wall of protection, the one who hurt you can't get in, but neither can those who can help.

> ✻ RECOVERY TIP:
> *When you protect yourself by building a wall, you're not only keeping out the one who hurt you, but also those who can help.*

Expending all this mental and emotional energy was exhausting me as Christmas neared, one of my favorite times of the year. I always enjoyed spending the holidays with my family in San Antonio, but this time I opted to stay in Dallas and work. I didn't think I could emotionally or spiritually handle being with them and possibly having to answer questions about my ex and the breakup. And in my wavering I still held out a foolishly romantic and unrealistic hope that he'd miss me so much around the holidays that we'd somehow reconcile.

Needless to say, I was incredibly disappointed when Christmas came and went without so much as a card or a phone call. I would have even been happy with an impersonal e-mail. Naturally, I was crushed that I was completely ignored by both my ex and his family. I just knew that at a time of the year when extra efforts are made to include friends and family in joyous celebrations of Christ's birth, a family of ministers like them would be more compassionate. How wrong I was!

I know this was one of those things that God just wanted me to accept, but my journal entries from this time show how hard this was for me.

Three days after thanking God for allowing me to be a blessing to others, I was wondering once again about the "why" of the situation. I thought I was crazy; my thoughts jumped from "Okay, I can handle this" to "God, why don't you just kill me and get the pain over with?" Still, I was making progress. The more I purposed to be emotionally and spiritually healthy, the harder it was to maintain my emotional and spiritual health. The more I wanted it, the more elusive it seemed to become.

During this time I prayed for endurance and the power to make it through. One friend who prayed with me and for me confirmed that God would allow me to make it through. She encouraged me to read the Scripture that says the winner is the one who endured and to trust that God would be with me in my valley of loneliness. Even though my emotions had me up one minute and down the next, I still wanted to believe that I could make it to wholeness.

One way I was able to endure was by developing stronger relationships with friends. I took a chance and leaned on a group of three for emotional and spiritual support. As a result, I grew more confident in my ability to have friends. Being abandoned and ignored by some friends during the first part of my recovery had disappointed and deeply wounded me. But as I grew in stronger relationships, these friends encouraged me with their constant affirmations. Their support also helped me deal with the emotional and spiritual hungers I was experiencing in my loneliness.

One of my favorite holiday memories as a child is baking sugar cookies with my mother. I would get excited, craving the taste of those soft and moist cookies melting in my mouth. It didn't really matter how each year's batch eventually turned out—and I get hungry now thinking about those cookies. It was merely my sweet memories of cookies past that fueled my hunger.

> **RECOVERY TIP:**
> *Hunger is a good thing—you are empty and need to be filled. You need to allow God to fill you with greater spiritual and emotional strength.*

Often during sentimental times, like the holidays, similar hungers and passions for past relationships affect us. For those of us suffering from a love hangover, the holidays can be both a time of hunger and a time of hope—a time of hunger for a lost relationship and a time of hope for the future to see how God will fill the void caused by the end of that relationship.

Hunger is a strong desire or discomfort rooted in a sense of lack or of not having enough. Emotionally, this can mean that although you may have lots of friends to socialize with, you still long for special times with that "oh so special" person. This is usually based on past memories of how fulfilling those times were.

On one hand, hunger is good because it reminds you that you are "empty" and need to be filled. It's God's way of reminding us that we need to allow him to fill us with the things he wants us to have. This includes greater emotional and spiritual characteristics like patience and peace. The problem with hunger arises when we try to satisfy it with something that is not good for us, for example, the "ex" or another romantic relationship.

These are some hungers that you might experience:

- Hunger for Acceptance. As hard as it is for you, you may notice that it is even harder for others to accept that your relationship has ended. It's natural to want others to support you and accept that the relationship is over. Try to not get frustrated at the comments of those who don't yet accept that the relationship failed. A few well-meaning friends told me that they were sure that my ex would attempt to reconcile with me during the holidays, if he really loved me. I'd rather these friends had given me loving support than false hope.

> **RECOVERY TIP:**
> *Recognize your hungers, especially the three A's: acceptance, attention, and affirmation—these are particularly hard to satisfy during a love hangover.*

- Hunger for Attention. The holidays bring so much attention to family and the importance of relationships. Resist the desire to place yourself in a relationship for the sake of being in one just so you can enjoy the attention that comes with it—especially if that person is not the best match for you emotionally, spiritually, and financially.

- Hunger for Affirmation. The rejection and abandonment you feel with a hangover is compounded by images on TV showing that we should all be happy with someone. Rarely do you see ads featuring happy single people enjoying the holidays. Resist the temptation to look to relationships for affirmation. Remind yourself that you are valuable whether or not you are in a romantic relationship. Surround yourself with safe people who will support you and not make you feel "less than" or as if you are missing out on life because you are single.

The hunger I felt as a child for those sugar cookies was my mind's and body's way of telling me to satisfy my physical hungers. Your emotional hungers during the holidays are a signal that you have a void that needs to be filled. Look at those hungers as a signal from God that you still have unmet emotional needs.

Hope comes with knowing that even during the darkest and loneliest times, God has not finished blessing you and is with you. Consider the void as God's way of reminding you that he desires to fill the voids in your emotional and spiritual life. Emotions, as uncomfortable as they are, form an important part of the bridge between us and God. The Scriptures say that he is touched by the "feeling" of our infirmity—it is through those feelings that God is touched and moved to act on our behalf.

Post-Love Hangover Reflection

A DIFFICULT PART OF MY LOVE HANGOVER was deciding to endure. I just wanted to stop and give up. Not because I didn't love God, but because I wasn't sure I loved myself enough. Looking back, I see that I had to go through this confusing part of the process, which felt like I was going in circles. It taught me that confusion can be a welcome part of the relationship recovery process. Fat that rises to the top after meat has cooled is much easier to scrape away. It gives the meat a special flavor, but in the end, it will lead to health problems if you digest too much of it. Confusion, which comes after the shock and anger have cooled, may comfort you during your recovery. However, if digested too much, confusion left in your life will lead to more severe emotional and spiritual problems. Like meat fat, God lets you see it so you can scrape it away.

Whispers of Love

Pause for Reflection

Signs You Are Suffering from a Love Hangover

1. You keep talking about your most recent relationship (the good or bad things) as though you are still together.
2. You still have some of your ex's clothes, pictures, jewelry, etc.
3. You make comparisons of your old relationship to your new one.
4. You call your ex just to see how he/she is doing or constantly ask other people how he/she is doing.
5. You have dreams, visions, and fantasies about revenge, and you actively strategize to break up your ex's new relationship.
6. You are unable to talk about the other person without crying or getting emotionally upset.
7. You find yourself listening to "your" song(s) and yearn for the relationship to be reconciled.
8. You avoid people and places that are reminders of your relationship (restaurants, movies).
9. You find it difficult to do normal things like go to work or school.
10. You still hope your ex will call.
11. You call your ex's home or jobs and hang up.

12. You drive by your ex's job or home hoping to catch a glimpse of him/her.
13. You fear and avoid intimacy and feel like you would rather die than be alone.
14. You now hate the opposite sex.
15. You avoid public places with the fear that you'll see your ex or someone you know.
16. You find it hard to envision your future and have lost sight of your goals.
17. You lose or gain weight and your sleeping patterns change.
18. You avoid exercising or become excessive and overexercise.
19. You stop caring for your personal appearance and hygiene.
20. Places that you normally keep clean (job, car, house) are now messy or dirty.

Describe a time when you've had to show courage in facing your fears and anger about your breakup.

So then, my beloved brethren,
let every man be swift to hear,
slow to speak, slow to wrath;
for the wrath of man does not produce
the righteousness of God.
James 1:19–20

Do you find yourself crying too much or not enough? Why?

Have I not commanded you?
Be strong and of good courage;
do not be afraid, nor be dismayed,
for the Lord your God
is with you wherever you go.
Joshua 1:9

How do you think that you've dealt with your anger and disappointment since your breakup? What is the biggest emotional challenge you've had to face concerning your breakup?

Those who sow in tears shall reap in joy.
Psalm 126:5

Out of the twenty signs listed, choose three that you are doing right now and write how you are going to stop doing them within the next twenty-one days.

For God has not given us a spirit of fear,
but of power and of love and of a sound mind.
2 Timothy 1:7

What three things about your relationship do you fear leaving behind?

Part 2

AFFIRMATION

My voice You shall hear
in the morning, O LORD;
In the morning
I will direct it to you,
And I will look up.

Psalm 5:3

"The simplest truths often meet the greatest resistance. . . ."
—*Frederick Douglass*

Affirmation helps to reframe and correct our thoughts. Affirmation only works, however, if it is true. At the same time, truth must be stated in present tense and said repetitiously either aloud or inwardly for our thinking and our behavior to be changed. Affirmation helps to shape behavior toward a goal. A runner might say "I am faster and faster each day" while visualizing herself crossing the finish line in first place. A person in recovery from a love hangover might say any of the following affirmations:

I have a good heart. I take good care of myself by eating properly, exercising regularly, and being a good steward over my finances. I easily accomplish my goals. I don't lie! I have the courage to say no when I mean no and to say yes when I mean yes. I communicate effectively with others. I never dwell on the past. I learn from my past mistakes and do better and better each day. I forgive myself. I am exciting, dynamic, and approachable. People are naturally attracted to the good in me. I do not run from intimate relationships. I have the courage to be vulnerable. I make healthy choices in the area of love relationship.

> *"When wisdom enters your heart,*
> *And knowledge is pleasant to your soul . . ."*
>
> Proverbs 2:10

Chapter 4

Living and Loving
in Moderation

*It is the second day of the New Year. What a transition!
I spent the last day of the old year seeking answers from
God. What does the New Year hold? What's in store for me
this year? The answer is transition, but from what to what?*

*I'm hopeful that God will respond to my prayer about
my emotions aligning with his will for my life. I'm now using
the time I am awakened at 3:00 A.M. to pray in the spirit. I
just wonder if my prayers are affective. . . . sometimes I don't
feel like it. God, why now? This is a very lonely time for me.
My good friends are either out of town or unavailable. I felt
awful, forgotten, and crushed to not receive a phone call
from my ex on Christmas or New Year's. I know I should be
over this but it still hurts. I wonder if I'm making progress.*

*I just wish people would stop saying that we're going
to reconcile . . . it breeds destructive false hope.*

*A few nights ago, I was in great anguish and very saddened
about it. I cried myself to sleep, again. I still miss him and*

being able to share my life with someone who cares. It's so sad to see what I once saw as love may not have been that at all. I've not forgiven him for all that he did to abruptly end our relationship. My prayer is that I will be able to forgive him and myself for what happened.

What is going on spiritually? I don't want to go church!

Today was a hard day. He made sure a few weeks ago to tell about his going-away reception at the church he works at. He also made sure not to invite me. I thought that this was cruel and cold for him to say those things and not invite me. Anyway, I drove by the church (not sure if it was by accident or on purpose) and the parking lot was full. My anger and tears come from him acting as though he is the only person who made an impact on the church during the time we dated. I worked three (albeit brief) weeks and also participated in their ministry and outreach programs. He even had me teach Bible study one night. It seems very selfish of him to not include me.

Reading my words, I look like a lunatic. It's so obvious that he doesn't give a damn—what a waste of a year and a half. Why is it that everybody I care about leaves me by myself?

As I prayed today, I could hear the Lord with my spiritual ears: The distance is not to hurt you but to protect you from what is coming. Be encouraged and know that I am with you; I have not forgotten you.

It hurts to feel so forgotten. My prayer, God, is that you would continue to align my feelings with your will for my life. I also pray, God, that you will give me peace during this season of hard emotion, loneliness, and obedience. I don't know what you are doing but can only pray that since you know what's best that you will use this experience for the best. Please, dear God, don't leave me too! Another Valentine's Day without any gifts . . . how frustrating!

Something has happened . . . my heart no longer feels that heavy burden and anguish of the heartbreak of abandonment. I realize now that I am so much stronger than I was two or three months ago. I still miss him and will probably always love him. I even promise to continue like I have been doing at night and pray for him when you wake me up at 3:00 A.M. He needs a different kind of friend/companion than who I am. My prayer for myself is that you, God, would continue to deliver me. Thank you for your faithfulness and for your never-ending love. Thank you for protecting me.

My feelings are back! The numbness is gone! I'm finally feeling a peace that surpasses my understanding of the situation.

L IKE MOST PEOPLE, I started the new year looking forward to the great things that would come my way. I wasn't sure what the new year promised, but I sure hoped that it was nothing like my previous year. Most of the entries from this month showed the definite emotional and spiritual strength that I was gaining. I had the momentum of newness to keep me pressing ahead.

However, there was one thing that I didn't know how to handle. Over those last few months, I had developed a closer walk with God and could hear his direction for my life clearer than ever. But I didn't want to go to church. How could this be? It seemed to me that the closer I got to God, the more I would want to spend time with his people. The opposite seemed to be happening. I wanted less and less to do with God's church people…or maybe it was just the ones that I knew.

I had to honestly admit that because my ex was an assistant pastor and most of our friends were in the ministry, I wanted nothing to do with people who were ministers. Just like I felt that my ex and his family were hypocrites, I began to wonder if others I knew in ministry were hypocrites as well. I knew it wasn't right to stereotype, but my ex was telling me that (1) God told him to end the relationship; (2) I hindered his ministry; and (3) had he known everything he learned about me before we dated, he never would have dated me, and it made me think that God also felt the same way about me.

Since I was a member of one of the fastest-growing megachurches in the country, I couldn't get a one-on-one appointment with my pastor. So I was stuck not wanting to go to church because of being distrustful of God's ministerial leaders. I also was embarrassed to go to church and answer continual questions about our relationship from others who didn't know that we'd broken up.

I made the effort and went to church a few times without having to answer these questions. However, one time I was asked and was given the cliché answer of God knowing best. Having heard that response dozens of times, I felt an overpowering urge to run from the room and rip my ears off. Being told that God knows best did nothing to take away my pain or dry my tears.

Because the wound was still very deep, I thought I wasn't making any progress. I wanted so desperately to stop crying every day. I wanted to stop thinking about him and what he was doing—and who he was doing it with. Only later did I realize that grief and relationship recovery is cyclical. I might have days of great sadness followed by a day of feeling triumphant. I kept telling myself that this was just part of the process.

> **RECOVERY TIP:**
> *You can't bargain with God. You can't express enough emotion or shed enough tears to bring about God's mercy and pity—God's unmerited grace is always there.*

I kept telling myself that I accepted the painful breakup, but at the same time, I was trying to bargain with God through my emotions. I was hoping if I shed enough tears, God would have great mercy and pity on me. Ultimately, I had to stop fighting the confusion. The bargaining part of the recovery process made me feel like I was still in limbo. But bargaining also kept me distracted from moving forward with the process, and in denial about the reality of the end of the relationship. I had to make a conscious decision to stop bargaining, because it was a waste of time and energy. When I did this, the shock and numbness I'd been feeling for three months went away. I was rejuvenated by a soothing and comforting peace. It wasn't a peace rooted in total acceptance, but it did give me the courage and freedom to let go of my favorite bargaining emotions like shock and disbelief. And with these growth steps, I was now ready to start letting go.

Another important step in the recovery process is letting go "gracefully." Grace, God's unmerited favor, gives us the chance to show maturity in how we handle the lessons of the truth. When we let go gracefully, the focus shifts from wanting to be right to wanting to move forward. One question I kept asking was, "Is it more important to be right or to be at peace? Sincere prayer was important to my making the transition to desiring peace.

Quite honestly, letting go gracefully was a huge struggle for me. I wavered between wanting to be Christlike and "live in peace," and wanting to slash my ex's new tires because my anger was justified. People agreed that he was wrong and that I was "right," but I still had no peace of mind. In fact, the more I settled on and became comfortable with being right, I had greater internal struggle—it didn't make sense that I was "right" and still couldn't sleep at night. My being hurt hadn't changed. I eventually got tired of being "right."

> **RECOVERY TIP:**
> *Letting go gracefully is an important step in getting through a love hangover. You shift the focus from wanting to be right to finding peace.*

As I prayed for peace of mind, the more I felt compelled to pray for him. Why would God ask me to pray for him? Maybe it was the devil. . . . In reality, this was a test to see if my great talk about being a Christian included extending grace through prayer. During this period I shed the most tears. I thought it was because of the memories of the pain, but it was because I was also being forced to grow—and that hurt! I honestly didn't think I could do it and not pray for God to "Get him, crush him, take the breath from him!" I had to discipline myself, listen closely to the voice of God, and pray accordingly.

I've often heard grace described as "getting what we don't deserve." Through prayer, I felt God extend grace to me and forgive me for the mistakes I made in the relationship and after the breakup. When I received the gift of God's grace, it was still difficult, but it became much easier for me to at least consider forgiving my ex. My insistence of being "right" didn't bring me closer to God. This attitude actually caused a breach in my intimate relationship with God because I wanted my ex to "earn" my forgiveness and apologize. Humbling myself through prayer did much to restrain my self-righteousness.

After praying for my ex, my thoughts softened. Understand, I still thought some evil, retaliatory things, but when I prayed, I would ask for God to help keep my mind like Philippians 4:8 states: *"Finally, brethren, whatever things are true, whatever things are noble, whatever things are just, whatever things are pure, whatever things are lovely, whatever things are of good report, if there is any virtue and if there is anything praiseworthy— meditate on these things."*

> ❋ RECOVERY TIP:
> *Pray for God's forgiveness for yourself and for your ex—it might not take away your hurt, but it will do wonders for your peace of mind.*

This time of prayer was the beginning of my change in attitude toward him. Because I prayed for him and knew that my thoughts were becoming more gracious and godly, I was able to respond pleasantly to people who unknowingly poured salt in the wound by asking about him. The circumstances hadn't changed, but my prayers for him had miraculously changed me.

Remember, to let go gracefully you should pray, pray, and then pray some more! Surround yourself with people who will pray for you as you struggle with this important part of Christian growth. Change who you talk to—the friends who are so willing to tear down your ex probably are not the best choice as you struggle with letting go gracefully. Pray for God to give you new friends, and he will. Change what you talk about—as difficult as it may be, limit your conversations about your ex.

This graceful period has no time limit—like the pain of a broken relationship, it can last as long or as short as you desire.

Post-Love Hangover Reflection

BARGAINING WAS A CHALLENGE because it kept me so distracted and believing that I wasn't going to ever make it out of the grief. I kept thinking that I would never get out of the emotional tug of war. I had to learn to rely on God, and this part of the process gave me more confidence in resting in his strength.

Chapter 5

Treasures of the Heart

Last night I didn't get much sleep . . . I think it's because I fought with God. There's a side of me that wants reconciliation. I'm mad at that side. There's also a side of me that wants nothing to do with my ex ever.

Is it out of anxiety and my fears that I now pray so desperately for deliverance and freedom? Please, dear God, I want to love and be loved. There's no freedom in confusion.

One of the fears that I realize I still struggle with is that a man will get to know me and then suddenly decide he doesn't want me. One of the more painful things my ex told me was that if he'd known what he eventually learned about me prior to dating, he'd never have started dating me. This hurts me especially because I'd previously shared with him how I struggled with a fear that once people get to know me, they won't like me. That's part of the reason why I don't like for people to get close. The sting of the rejection of strangers is nothing compared to that of people, like family and friends, who turn away from you.

I am now looking back with healthier eyes and look forward with great anticipation to the future. I wonder what impact this toxin from this relationship will have on my future romantic relationships. I'm going to have to work hard to dispel this fear that when a man doesn't call, it doesn't mean he's not interested. In the past, being concerned about this would have kept me stuck in the endlessly tormenting cycle of go away, come closer. There is no way to work through this fear without being in relationship with others. It takes working on my faith in God, trusting of others, and building my esteem.

I talked to a friend about my fears of reconciling with my ex. His response: "Reconciliation is not restoration."

E VEN THOUGH I WROTE these journal entries just a few days apart, there is such a contrast to the feelings expressed. I was still reeling from my ex's rejection, but I knew that I would make it through. I'd had a broken heart before and knew that I would be able to recover.

When I was asked by someone what I wanted from my ex, my immediate response was, "NOTHING!" He's not willing to give me anything valuable. I realized that I'd matured and had accepted that I couldn't be married to him.

I was willing to reconcile because as Christians we should not have strife separating us, but I knew that I didn't want to be in a close relationship with him ever again. He was so cold after we broke up that I don't think I could even trust him or feel comfortable around him. I struggled with reconciliation because I thought it meant that we'd have to get back together. Even though part of my heart still loved him, I didn't want that. I knew I wasn't in danger of going back to him if the opportunity ever arose. The hurt woman in me still wanted to tell him, "No thanks!"

The sudden collapse of my emotional support system was also crippling. The comfort I would have gotten from church family was nonexistent, and my real family was hundreds of miles away. Being by myself so much during this time was overwhelming. The few friends I could share with were either working or out of town, so I didn't see them often. Other than people at my job or students in my class, I had very little contact with anybody else. Friendships had always been important to me, and I began to treasure them even more.

> **RECOVERY TIP:**
> *Friendships are important—you have friends and they will challenge you to assess and reassess what you want and what you need from them.*

I kept hearing my ex's words, "I'll be your friend. I mean, if your car breaks down on the freeway and you can't reach anybody else, you can then call me." He knew when he said those words that, having lived here a short amount of time, I knew very few people. And I was naturally cautious about who I became good friends with. The few friends that I confided in didn't know it, but they were challenging me to assess and reassess what I really wanted from my friends.

The Bible is full of stories and examples of great friendships. Ruth and Naomi, David and Jonathan, Mary, Martha, Lazarus, and Jesus. Jesus referred to his disciples as friends in John 15:15: "*But I have called you friends, for all things that I have heard of my Father I have made known unto you.*" In fact, the term "friend" is mentioned fifty-three times in the Bible.

During my love hangover I grasped the importance of my friends. Like Proverbs 27:9 states: "*Ointment and perfume rejoice the heart, so doth the sweetness of a man's friend by hearty counsel.*" Even though I wasn't up to talking to a great deal of people about my emotional state, I did open up to a few. I struggled with choosing which ones I could safely confide in. I struggled over which ones had my best interests at heart. Unfortunately, some deceived me, even in my time of heartbreak. After I got over the hurt from the lies, I was able to thank God for revealing the true nature of that friendship and accept that, like Zechariah 13:6: "*I was wounded in the house of my friends.*"

> **RECOVERY TIP:**
> *Accept the fact that the holidays will be painful after a breakup—pray for strength and endurance, and lean on some of your friends for support.*

It was also during this time that I found out that a good friend was gay. Her former lover told me this shocker because of her own hurt at being dumped by her. My shock was not about my friend being gay, but about the betrayal of the friendship. Not Again! I screamed on the inside. She was a minister and I had relied on her for counsel and for a shoulder to cry on. I was very angry at the thought of another betrayal. I had confided a number of things to her during the breakup, only to learn later that she'd been in constant communication with my ex.

I lost my ex as a lover, and I also lost him as a friend. I know that romantic feelings change, but it was hard to see how someone could so easily go from being your friend one day to your very public and bitter enemy the next. This forced me to look at my definition of friendship. It was difficult to deal with those who had conveniently detached themselves from me with the excuse, "We like both of you. We don't want to take sides." I didn't want them to take sides, but I thought that they should at least empathize.

Be still, and know that I am God!

Psalm 46:10

Without many friends to whom I could turn, I grew to better appreciate silence, and specifically God's silence. I read once that we should treasure God's silence because it shows that he can trust us. At first, I didn't understand it because I was going through a painfully quiet time of praying to God and waiting on a response.

I didn't actually expect to hear an audible voice respond to my concerns, but I also didn't expect to hear the deafening silence and feel such a void. I had to keep believing, even through the silence, that God was with me, even when I couldn't feel his presence.

> ✳ RECOVERY TIP:
> *Appreciate and treasure silence. Silence doesn't have to be deafening and painful—it may signify a higher level of trust and a maturing of your relationship with God.*

Think about how your parents, your boss, and your partner show you that they trust you. Not by hounding you and watching your every move, but by giving you the freedom to live, work, and love. Your parents showed they trusted you when they let you stay in the house by yourself for a weekend and didn't call to check up on you every hour. Your boss shows that he/she trusts you by going on vacation and not calling back every day. Your significant other shows that he/she trusts you by not calling or paging you every hour when you go out of town.

God deals with us in very much the same way. His silence as we wait for answers to prayers is his way of showing us that he trusts us to handle the growth that it requires. Silence signifies a higher level of trust and signifies that the relationship is maturing for the benefit of all involved. Sometimes his protection in silence is his shielding us from things, experiences, and people that don't have our best interests at heart.

Post-Love Hangover Reflection

IN RADIO BROADCASTING, silence is known as "dead air." Who came up with the phrase, I don't know, but dead air is not good for radio because it means that there has been a mistake, either by the equipment or by the on-air personality. Whatever the cause, the immediate response is to correct it so that those listening can continue to enjoy the station. Sometimes it's not easily corrected and you just have to wait until the situation corrects itself.

I had to take the same perspective on "dead air" in my prayer life. I thought that there was a reason why God hadn't answered my prayers for friends, and then I tried to correct it by changing my prayers. I didn't realize that he had answered my prayers for friends by separating me from people who weren't my friends. Spiritual growth has changed my prayers. Sometimes the "dead air" is more than just an opportunity for me to fine tune my prayer requests. God's silence is his way of showing me that (1) he trusts me and (2) he protects me.

Chapter 6

Is That Your Final Answer?

I no longer feel that nervousness I felt when this breakup began. I'm still saddened by the loss but realize that even in distress, God is protecting me. I haven't seen him in three months—strange since we live less than five minutes from each other. I thank you for giving me peaceful rest.

WHEN I WROTE THIS, I was still having trouble sleeping but was finally beginning to accept the peace that God was mercifully offering me, like he states in Psalm 91. But even as I was trying to grasp onto the peace, I made a conscious effort to avoid driving down certain streets. I was not sure how I would respond if I ran into my ex or ran into him with another woman. I didn't have any proof, but I just felt like he was already in a relationship with someone else.

Something I learned to use as a spiritual tool when I was a member of the New Creation Christian Fellowship Church in San Antonio was the combination of prayer and fasting. I was not ashamed to admit that I wanted something from God. I didn't want my ex back, but I sure wanted him out of my emotional system.

But simply wanting him out of my system wasn't working. I decided to try fasting and intensified periods of prayer—two to three hours at a time. Fasting also meant spending more uninterrupted time with God, limiting my television viewing time, and listening exclusively to praise and worship/gospel music.

> **RECOVERY TIP:**
> *Consider a spiritual cleansing. Limit your television viewing time and abstain from meats and sweets for a month—but do it with the purpose of committing yourself to God and to yourself.*

I didn't think that a month of fasting would be that difficult because I'd lost my appetite since the breakup. Some days I had to tell myself, "You will eat today." The stress of the initial breakup plus the mild depression that followed affected my appetite. Within a few months, my usually healthy appetite had returned, which was a sign that I was well on my way to restoration.

My next phase of recovery involved cleansing myself and my spiritual "house." I went on a monthlong fast, prayed intently, and asked others to pray for me. I also went to counselors. These ended up being the best investments I could make in my emotional and spiritual state.

I went on a "Daniel fast" and abstained from all meats and sweets for the month of February. I know it sounds brutal and unhealthy, but imagine a healthy diet of fruits and vegetables for twenty-nine days. My sentiments exactly—yuck! Being a junk-foodaholic, I nearly backslid during this period.

My Christian experience had taught me that when you really want God to move mightily on your behalf, and prayer doesn't seem to be working, fasting catches God's attention and, in many ways, shows a deeper commitment. During previous fasts, I'd received news like being admitted to graduate school and new jobs, so I figured getting a man out of my system wouldn't be that big of a deal. This fast was difficult not because I gave up fried chicken, but because of what I was fasting about. I was so tormented by thoughts of him, what he was doing, and who was he doing it with.

The Daniel fast is taken from the biblical passage found in Daniel, chapter 1:8–20:

> *But Daniel resolved not to defile himself*
> *with the royal food and wine, and he asked the chief official*
> *for permission not to defile himself this way.*
> *Now God had caused the official*
> *to show favor and sympathy to Daniel,*
> *but the official told Daniel, "I am afraid of my lord the king,*
> *who has assigned your food and drink. Why should he*
> *see you looking worse than the other young men your age?*
> *The king would then have my head because of you."*
> *Daniel then said to the guard whom the chief official had*
> *appointed over Daniel, Hananiah, Mishael, and Azariah,*
> *"Please test your servants for ten days:*
> *Give us nothing but vegetables to eat and water to drink.*
> *Then compare our appearance with that of the young men*
> *who eat the royal food, and treat your servants*
> *in accordance with what you see."*
> *So he agreed to this and tested them for ten days.*
> *At the end of the ten days they looked healthier*
> *and better nourished than any of the young men*
> *who ate the royal food. . . .*
> *To these four young men God gave knowledge and*
> *understanding of all kinds of literature and learning.*
> *And Daniel could understand visions and dreams of all kinds. . . .*

The king talked with them, and he found none equal
to Daniel, Hananiah, Mishael, and Azariah;
so they entered the king's service.
In every matter of wisdom and understanding
about which the king questioned them, he found them ten times
better than all the magicians and enchanters
in his whole kingdom. (NIV)

After my fast, I began to see things more clearly and felt emotionally stronger. My feelings were still very strong but I was now able to do things like go to the grocery store and not bristle at the thought of seeing him or someone from his church. In fact, since I was going to the store for my "veggies," I was more focused on slipping up and buying my favorite Oreos.

I also "fasted" from distracting TV and radio programs. I committed to spending my non-work-related time to talking with God and praying for him to show me the next steps. This meant that I didn't watch anything other than the news (but that was work-related). No sitcoms, movies, or anything that timewise would draw me away from God.

I also did not listen to secular music during this fasting period. I have a good supply of gospel music handy, and so I stocked my car with music from my most inspiring gospel music artists. My personal favorite was Fred Hammond and Radical for Christ's "The Inner Court," based on "Philippians 4:7," with its lyrics about God giving a peace that surpasses understanding. I was tormented by thoughts of what I had done so wrong to deserve such mean and cruel treatment by my ex and his family/friends. I really needed to hear that God could give me a peace. This is what I was searching for and what I needed to be daily reminded of.

By not listening to the other kinds of music, I forced my mind and spirit to constantly focus on the things of God. The sweet aroma of the praise music kept my spirit open to hearing God. I didn't want to miss any opportunity to hear him concerning my situation.

Yesterday I cried. Last night, I cried out to God to heal me of my tormenting thoughts of him and also the shame I feel about being rejected. I guess I cried out of frustration because it seems like it's taking so long. I know, God, that you have many blessings for me—I just wonder why this release couldn't have happened in November when the breakup took place. When I pray I hear "Not yet." Well, why not? He's not made any move to contact me. I want my full night's rest and I want to be able to love again (and be married).

This is four months to the day since my ex "heard" God tell him that we needed a two month separation. It's been more than two months and it's been a period of great growth, most which I fought. Like having to pray for him, not feeling like I was truly free, dealing with the shock and the emotional trauma.

This is my last fast day. I thank you, God, for shielding me during this time. You are continuing to answer my prayers and restoring me to wholeness. I no longer have the desire of a few months back to be his wife or to have him as a part of my life. All trust and respect for him are gone.

I BELIEVE THAT THE COMBINATION of fasting and prayer actually sped up the recovery process. I was beginning to feel like I did before I started dating him—more free and confident in my judgment concerning men. I hadn't grasped how much the relationship had negatively affected my self-esteem until I needed it to strengthen me during this time.

> RECOVERY TIP:
> *Prayer and fasting won't change the situation, but they will change you— you may even find yourself praying for your ex and letting go.*

Yet even in the triumph of my emotional stability returning, I had to deal with tormenting thoughts and feeling like I was still connected to him. I was definitely ready to move on, but I felt burdened by the memories of our relationship. I used to think I was crazy because I knew he was moving on without me—and still I loved him!

Several times during my month of fasting, I found myself wide awake at 3:00 A.M. with a great urge to pray for my ex. The first time it happened, I admit, I refused, and tried in vain to go back to sleep. Two hours later I was still awake, and in exasperation I asked God why I needed to pray for him, a minister, when he had plenty of other people praying for him. I didn't get a response, and by then it was time to go to work.

The next night when it happened, I wondered why God would have me pray for someone who had hurt me so badly. I mean, there was no guarantee that I'd pray anything nice or holy for him. The following night, again at the same time, I simply asked God, "What am I supposed to pray?" Then I received greater clarity on what to pray and was able to earnestly pray on his behalf.

Even after four months, it seemed like I hadn't made much progress. To me, progress would have meant having no thoughts whatsoever about my ex. God obviously had another plan.

I didn't know it then, but one of the benefits of my increased prayer time was a sharpened discernment in hearing God. Prayer didn't change the situation, but it sure did change me.

Post-Love Hangover Reflection

ATTITUDE ADJUSTMENT is one of the most difficult lessons for me to learn in my spiritual growth. One of my mistakes was that I had put more faith in my prayers than in the God who answers prayers. Prayer affirmed who I was in God's eyes, that he trusted me and wanted to hear from me. Like any loving father, he gave me extra responsibility through prayer and fasting. He showed me at a time when I needed it most that he valued me, even when others didn't. Spending time in prayer helped me achieve the necessary attitude adjustment.

Whispers of Love

Pause for Reflection

Slipped Away

I was slipped away in the pain you put me in yesterday.
I was slipped away in the pain and my heart almost rotted away.
But I finally came to realize you're not the one for me.
I finally came to realize what I once couldn't see.
Although I love you dearly, our love must come to an end.
Although I love you dearly in my heart we're still friends.
But for a moment I slipped away in the pain
but I won't do it again
because you're not worth the tears.

Tracy A. Mayfield (© 2000)

Thinking about the words of the poem, describe a painfully anxious moment concerning your breakup.

The discretion of a man makes him slow to anger,
And his glory is to overlook a transgression.

Proverbs 19:11

How did the breakup positively or negatively affect
your friendships?

> *Faithful are the wounds of a friend,*
> *But the kisses of an enemy are deceitful.*
> Proverbs 27:6

Name at least one thing that you felt ashamed about after a
relationship breakup. Describe how you feel God helps you with
your shame.

> *Be anxious for nothing, but in everything*
> *by prayer and supplication, with thanksgiving,*
> *let your requests be made known to God.*
> Philippians 4:6–7

How have you used affirmation and endurance to sustain you
through your lowest emotional valley?

> *Oh, taste and see that the LORD is good;*
> *Blessed is the man who trusts in Him!*
> Psalm 34:8

What do you have a spiritual hunger for?

Part 3

CONFIDENCE

But I will sing of Your power;
Yes, I will sing aloud
of Your mercy in the morning;
For You have been my defense
And refuge in the day of my trouble.

Psalm 59:16

> "IF YOU HAVE NO CONFIDENCE IN SELF,
> YOU ARE TWICE DEFEATED IN THE RACE
> OF LIFE. WITH CONFIDENCE YOU HAVE
> WON EVEN BEFORE YOU HAVE STARTED."
> —*Marcus Garvey*

On some level, when faced with the reality that love has failed in a relationship, a fight ensues. In one corner there is the truth—love never fails. In the other corner is the false reality—love has failed you. In believing the falsehood that love has failed you, all efforts to try again seem futile. What's the point of entering a situation where you feel doomed to failure? And believing that love has failed and will fail you, you are truly setting up the course for disappointment. Have confidence in yourself. Believe and know for certain that whatever you did or did not do, whatever you said or did not say, you did the best you could at the time. And now, with the confidence gained from the experience of your past, you are better equipped—not less equipped—to try once again.

*I can do all things through Christ
who strengthens me.*

Philippians 4:13

Chapter 7

Betrayal by
Any Other Name

---

*Today I found out he was marrying someone else. I can't
believe it. Not that he can't fall in love with someone else
but that it would be so soon after we broke up. It really
makes me question a lot of things about myself, him, and
you, God. Why did I have to pray for him so long? Why
couldn't he just tell me the truth? Why the need to be so
deceptive? Why such a lack of respect for my feelings?
What did I do to deserve this treatment? It makes me
question all of the reasons he said he ended the relationship—he felt trapped and angry. Did he not trust me
enough to be honest? How long had he been dating her?
The really bad part is that he told other people two months
ago about him getting married—and he didn't tell me!*

WHEN I WROTE THIS JOURNAL ENTRY, I felt a strange sense
of both freedom and pain. It was just plain awful and
emotionally brutalizing to hear that man that I still loved and cared

for was so joyful about marrying another woman. I felt cheated because he'd told me and his church congregation just nine months earlier that he was planning to marry me.

Never had I felt so disrespected by someone. He should have at least respected my feelings and told me personally. He was so open and cocky about his wedding plans. Even more humiliating is that I found out on the day I was scheduled to sing at a church program at his seminary. Had I known, I wouldn't have subjected myself to that embarrassment.

> RECOVERY TIP:
> *You will have setbacks. You will have doubts. You will wonder who else is betraying you—and you will come to the understanding that some questions will never be answered.*

In spite of the great progress I'd made (I'd even stopped journaling for a while), this news knocked the emotional wind out of me. It took everything I had to not burst into tears while I was singing "God Will Take Care of You." As I was singing, I thought, "But you haven't taken care of me, God." Now, after months of progress, I was back to crying myself to sleep again.

When it became obvious that other friends knew about his marriage at least two months earlier and hadn't told me, I wondered who else was betraying me. I thought I'd accepted the fact that some questions would never be answered. Yet this bit of news opened a floodgate of more questions. My inquisitive and analytical nature took over and I was tormented daily by a barrage of unanswered questions.

I still have so many questions. Why couldn't he be honest? Why didn't I see the change? Who is she? Why does he love her more than me? Why doesn't his family like me? Did they ever like me? Why did they pretend? I realize that these questions will never be answered. It's unfair because I may never know what I did to cause the end of the relationship.

This is why it is important for me to continue the path to wholeness. My desire is that my sessions with my counselor will prove successful in closing the still open emotional doors. The last six months have been emotionally draining, physically challenging, and spiritually wearying. I pray that I just don't quit.

Strangely, I remember the sense of relief that I felt when I found out—like a burden was lifted. Again, it's strange, considering that I still love him. It hurts to see other people look at me like I'm a some kind of wounded animal. When they find the courage to talk to me about it, they tell me things that he said about our relationship. Why does he have to lie? It's not necessary.

A PHRASE I HEARD OFTEN after the breakup was, "You really shouldn't question God. You should just accept what he allows." Maybe I'm still that hardheaded and curious child who drove my parents crazy, but I found it difficult not to ask questions during my recovery period. I had faith that God would turn my pain around for something good, but I still had a lot of questions and expected answers. Sometimes I felt that my faith wasn't strong enough to just accept the circumstances in my life. Looking at biblical examples showed me that asking questions is important because it builds the type of intimate relationship where the truth can be revealed.

The ministerial life of Jesus was characterized by the many questions that were posed to him by the Pharisees, Sadducees, and his own disciples. During many of these "Q and A" sessions Jesus was able to explain a number of things, including his purpose and God's plan for humanity. Jesus is often depicted as enjoying the opportunity to respond to their questions and lead them to the truth. As a result of their boldness, Jesus established more intimate relationships with those disciples closest to him.

> **RECOVERY TIP:**
> *You will experience greater intimacy in your relationship with God and with others when you can humbly admit to yourself that you didn't know it all.*

Similarly, I had to realize that it was okay to boldly ask God questions. At first, I thought God would bellow with a loud voice that he was the great "I AM" and that I was just hardheaded and needed to stop asking stupid questions when the answers were obvious. The responses I got when I asked questions like "Why did this happen?" and "How could I have been so foolish?" granted me peace. The peace came not in the answers to my questions but in the increased intimate time of prayer and meditation. My confidence was restored as I learned through this process that I could take all of my concerns to God.

Because of my pride, I struggled greatly even asking those questions, because I thought that as a Christian I knew the answer: I should just accept what happened and have faith that God knew what was best for me. However, only after I asked questions and admitted that I didn't have all the answers did I begin to develop a better relationship with God. It was truly an act of humility to ask a question because I was forced to admit to myself and others what they already knew: I didn't know it all!

Once I admitted this, I began to experience greater intimacy in my relationship with God and others. I was no longer able to hide behind a mask of "having all the answers." Like John 8:32 states, "And ye shall know the truth, and the truth shall make you free," the risk I took in asking questions was rewarded by the freedom of knowing the truth.

I was challenged to be more open to relationships, and guess what? I did it by opening myself to him, and I got hurt in the process. What kind of reward is that? Despite all of this, I realize I have been spared and protected from an unhealthy, destructive, and regressive relationship. Why do I still shed tears? Why are my cheeks still wet? Why do I still lament the.loss of something that was not good for me? Why do I still have questions?

I'M AMAZED AT HOW MUCH I realize now that I didn't want to see about our relationship. His ability to remain emotionally cool and calm, which I admired, was actually his inability to effectively express his emotions. At this point, I was starting to accept that our relationship had many problems that were never addressed. Not because we didn't want to; neither one of us really knew how to address issues without hurting each other's feelings. Now, I believe that even if the problems had been addressed, they wouldn't have changed the outcome.

I have learned that it was okay to be angry; it was okay to feel that I had received mixed signals from him. It wasn't wise to act on those feelings, but feeling them was healthy. My ex often encouraged me not to express my feelings. I didn't realize it but it was a crafty tool of manipulation that stifled intimacy with myself, others, and, most importantly, God.

Once I accepted the reality of the situation—that some dreams that I had for us would never come true and promises he had made, like marrying me, would remain broken—I could accept the feelings of guilt, shame, and rejection. I was also able to shake off the ghosts from my childhood that told me that to have feelings was not okay. I thought that emotions cut you off from people.

> **RECOVERY TIP:**
> *It's okay to get angry. Not expressing emotions is a form of manipulation—it stifles intimacy with yourself, with others, and with God.*

I was making small steps of growth, but I sometimes felt the depth of the pain. If a heart attack is worse than this, I pray to God I never have one. To even think of having to relive such heartache and pain, such anguish, such disappointment, such disgust is beyond my imagination. I am tired of these tears that I have tasted night after night and waking up to countless empty boxes of tissue. I am sleep deprived and angry at myself for being so vulnerable.

Many times I have stood at the bathroom mirror, bargaining and blaming myself, searching for imperfections. I'm sick of trying to justify and ease the pain. It's too painful to look deep inside what is left of my wounded soul for answers to so many questions. Answers to questions I am forced to answer. You see, there was never any closure. This is my story. Yours may read like this:

I walked in on them. I stood there in disbelief, thinking, "Somebody slap me, because this can't be true! How could he? Hasn't he seen at least one of those music videos with this scene? Doesn't every person who cheats on his lady have the common sense and decency not to bring their `other love' home?" I stood in sheer disbelief and exhaled. The signs were always there. I just chose not to acknowledge them.

Why? We had spent seven years together, and I passed on job promotions in other cities. I was dedicated to him and only him. I rubbed the back of my neck with one hand and rested the other on the cherrywood bedpost. I had to keep my hands occupied as I came to grips with this discovery. Naked and drenched in sweat, he buried his head under the pillow in shame. She grabbed what she could: skirt, pumps, and bra, and left. She made no attempt to defend her lustful actions. It's ironic. Even though my heart felt so empty and lifeless, it pounded like never before. She couldn't even look me in the eye as she passed me. Amazed at what I was realizing, my disgust behind such an act of betrayal magnified.

This is only one scenario. They are all devastating for a number of reasons. Not only are you forced to deal with the relationship ending but you have to come to grips with the knowledge that you really didn't know the person you were dating. You are forced to realize that you have been "living a lie." Hurt and perplexed, you think:

"Why would he lead me on . . . telling me, his friends, and his mother I was the one and then. . . ."

"What kind of girl can seem so dedicated to two hearts at the same time and. . . ."

"But he seemed so sincere. So genuine. I have dated players before and I thought I could see them coming a mile away but. . . ."

Or you may have experienced a failed relationship where you had to deal with the shock of the breakup but there were no morality issues or disappointing character flaws in your mate.

"Everything was so perfect. We both gave our all, loving each other unconditionally. No days, sunny or cloudy, without 'I love you.' No question of infidelity. Our relationship was even envied by our friends."

> **RECOVERY TIP:**
> *Accept the fact that you will never realize 100 percent "what went wrong" —especially if there is no closure to the relationship and no honest communication with your ex.*

"We made it a point to put God first in our relationship. With him as our foundation it had to pass the test of time. We went to singles Bible study together, choir rehearsal every Thursday and, of course, church every Sunday. I just don't understand why."

"I prayed to God to bring me the right person. A God-fearing man. Someone God would have me be with. I promised him I was in no hurry, that I would be patient. I promised myself I would not be influenced by external beauty. And I wasn't. What he drove, where he worked, his financial status—none of that mattered. He was my soulmate, and he was all that I prayed for and more. Why would God let such a man enter my life only to leave me? Where did I go wrong?"

In the rebuilding process, you have to realize that you may never attain a complete understanding of "what went wrong," especially if there is no closure and your ex will not discuss it with you. He probably was either not totally honest with himself, not totally honest with you, in denial with possibly repressed and internalized issues, or any combination of the three. Maybe she didn't tell you six months ago she wanted to see other people because she wasn't really 100 percent sure. Once you say it . . . remember you can't take it back. Maybe he initially thought his days of playing the field were in his past, but midstream he began to question his faithfulness and true dedication. He knows he has a beautiful, dedicated, faithful woman with hopes of eventual matrimony. But now he faces the resurfacing of a demon—craving other women.

Seeking understanding can be spiritually challenging. We assume that we know exactly God's purpose and intentions, in a sense, having the script in hand, reading along. "Okay, God allowed this to happen, but I don't understand why he would let me be so disappointed and heartbroken!" This is not the case; don't be confused. God often allows things to happen in our lives so we will gain understanding and attain wisdom.

This has been an interesting week. I've been very emotional and wondering what's next. I'm having a very difficult time seeing you, God, in this whole thing. Not that you aren't with me, but I'm mad at your leaders, God. They are supposed to be your representatives on earth, but they have no standard other than their own that they follow. I need to stop saying that this situation did not affect me spiritually, because it did. I'm in spiritual limbo because I don't want to trust men of God anymore. My ex comes from a family of preachers and yet you allow them to abuse the body of Christ! Why don't you stop them, God? They are supposed to protect but instead they use and take advantage. I feel disconnected

*from you, God. You have proven yourself to me throughout
this time and I should be more trusting.*

*I wonder if he ever valued what we shared as friends
and lovers. What is it about her that makes him act so
mean toward me? What is it about me that doesn't know
how to meet and successfully deal with men? I didn't go
to my prom, I'm divorced—why do thoughts of abandonment pain me so? It's like to some people I don't exist
without my ex.*

M Y BELIEFS ABOUT WHO God was and wasn't and why I saw
him this way were frustrating me at this point. In a rela-
tively short amount of time, I'd grown so much emotionally, yet I
still wanted to understand more about who God was. I'd learned
more about myself. The realization that I was afraid of social situations shocked me. I always thought that I was extroverted, but my
life was actually indicating something different. At first I thought it
was people. I was relieved to know that it was how we socialized
that actually scared me.

I tried to break out of the habit of spending the majority of
my time by myself. I was now feeling that my great social experiment failed. I had not met all of my goals for change, but I kept
trying. I didn't want others to see me for the loser that I still
sometimes felt like I was. It was merely an aftereffect of the
rejection by my ex.

I was trying my social experiment one more time when I
accepted an invitation for lunch from an obviously anxious friend.
Imagine my surprise when she told me that she and another close
friend of mine, Sherry, were actually lovers. I'd had my suspicions

but didn't want to jump to conclusions. She then confided her anger and fears to me. She'd just been dumped and thought I could give her a sympathetic ear.

I was really trying to listen to her, but I couldn't get beyond the statement that they were gay. I wasn't so much concerned about the homosexuality as I was about Sherry lying to me about it and lying about her having communicated with my ex. Sherry was also a minister and had very graciously offered a shoulder for me to cry on after the breakup. Despite her offer and the fact that I shared many of my times of deepest pain with her, the five-year friendship obviously meant more to me than it did to her.

> **RECOVERY TIP:**
> *Trust in new friend-ships. Rejection tends to make you turn in on yourself—break the habit of isolating yourself that you've developed during your love hangover.*

This just reminded me of lessons I learned during the first part of my love hangover about the true character of my friends and whether or not they had good intentions. It disappointed me when friends who had been very open when I was part of a dating couple became very distant after the breakup. I had to decide what I was going to do now that I saw the false nature of those friends. I struggled with whether I could still consider them friends if they avoided me and my painful emotional issues. The answer became clearer as I found Scripture passages relating to friends and friendships, like Proverbs 18:24: "A friend loves at all times, And a brother is born for adversity."

Part of the intense pain I felt from the breakup was because I loved my ex as a friend and missed his friendship more than anything else. His response when I told him that I wanted to reconcile our friendship about a month after our breakup was that he still considered me his friend—I was just one of his friends that he'd never call. I was so crushed because it reminded me of when my best friend in the sixth grade also rejected my friendship. I hadn't dealt with that loss, and now I found myself feeling empty and lost like I had twenty years earlier. It was now time for me to deal with these issues.

God then placed people in my life who were truly concerned about my emotional and spiritual health. They made sure that I knew I could call them any time of the day or night. They sometimes called me at odd times late at night, just to make sure I was doing okay or to pray with me. Ironically, though I was unhappy, I was so comfortable with my solitude that the constant communication often conflicted with my desire for my "safe" isolation. I figured that they would get tired of hearing me complain and cry and would reject me, so I started to reject their attempts at friendship. I wanted to keep my feelings to myself, but I had to admit that I felt much better when I was able to share them with others.

Their persistence forced me to realize that a good support system is essential to having a successful recovery. My past feelings of distrust were challenged by my friends who gave me safe places to vent my anger, frustration, sorrow and despair. Proverbs 27:9 states: "Ointment and perfume delight the heart, And the sweetness of a man's friend gives delight by hearty counsel."

Out of fear and embarrassment, I wanted to isolate myself from others. But by allowing myself to trust in these new friendships, God was able to rebuild my character and began to restore my self-esteem. Knowing that I had a circle of support gave me the confidence to walk through the steps to wholeness.

Post-Love Hangover Reflection

MY LOVE HANGOVER MADE ME REALIZE that feelings can connect you with safe people and that it is healthy to feel. God connects with us through our emotions. Sometimes when I find myself caught in the today pain of a yesterday experience, I say, "I may feel bad today, but I'm going to feel just a little better tomorrow." At times, I was discouraged because I thought I'd be doing better at a certain point. I focused so much on the "time" and what God was doing with it that I didn't allow him to do what he wanted with my feelings. So even though I felt like I was in limbo because I was still crying at night and very lonely, I was actually allowing God to heal me and change my emotions.

> RECOVERY TIP:
> *Having a circle of support gives you the confidence to walk toward wholeness. When someone rejects you, it's their problem, not yours.*

I learned a good lesson that when others reject me, it's their problem, not mine. Keeping this in mind gives me the boldness to enter new social situations without the fear of rejection.

As a result of my love hangover, I have stopped seeing God as some Wizard of Oz manipulating others and me from behind the scenes. I now see him as a loving, balanced God who wants his children to be the same. My pain has forced me out of my comfort zone. I was so safe in my behaviors and beliefs that I fought accepting the more mature belief that God loves me even when he doesn't give me what I want. As he has changed my view of him, he has also changed my view of myself.

Chapter 8

Letting Go Gracefully . . .

Today I destroyed the birthday, anniversary, and other special greeting cards and pictures that my ex gave me over the course of our relationship. Before I ripped each one up, I read it. Rereading the cards reminded me of the time when he gave me the cards and we were so much in love. Painful memories still, but I had to face them. I can't pretend like him, that those feelings were wrong or never existed. Nor can I pretend that the relationship wasn't a special part of my life. Lately, I've been struggling with his statements that our relationship never should have taken place and that people were wrong who wanted us to get married. These thoughts bring up so many feelings of rejection and guilt and shame over being rejected.

Please forgive me, God, for allowing me to feel this way. Please, dear God, forgive me for being mad at you for allowing this to happen. I've been so angry and felt justified in telling you how unfair you were to let those two marry. I mean, why couldn't you break them up like we were broken up? I realize that like Job, I must deal with the four

Ws (what, when, where, who) and not the whys of my relationship ending. I'm also still so hurt about my friend's betrayal—I can't believe I was that naive.

I guess I was holding onto the pictures so I could prove that our relationship did exist, if I needed to them show in the future. However, my ex and I both know what we shared. Though he has chosen to twist and demonize the relationship, it doesn't change the reality of what the relationship was.

By dealing with the reality of what was, I can now move into the future. It's weird, but in my loneliness, those cards kept me company. I'm still lonely but desire the peace that only comes in moving toward a healthy future.

Today I saw a picture of my ex's new wife in the bridal section of the newspaper. My response was weird. After seeing it, I didn't cry or scream; I just lost my appetite and stopped eating my chicken tamale. I'm puzzled by my response—shouldn't I be upset or crying or something? Shouldn't I want to storm to the church he is now pastoring and create an embarrassing scene? I'm not really numb— that implies shock, and I'm not shocked.

I FELT SO EXHILARATED when I finally was able to embrace the memories of the relationship without feeling like I was in bondage. Some people who had known both of us simply now acted like our relationship never existed. They avoided saying his name or talking about anything that occurred in my life while we were dating. So I felt like I had to prove that our love had existed.

By throwing away those cards, I was letting go of the idea that I had to prove anything.

A gripping part of a love hangover is being controlled by others' thoughts and opinions. In my mind, the cards would prove to anybody that I wasn't some sick, lovelorn exgirlfriend and that he had often openly expressed his love for me. He had given me gifts, cards, and other expressions of love.

One day the Lord placed it on my heart to reread the cards that my ex had given me. At first I thought this was crazy and would cause me great pain. The cards were in a bag inside my closet and I had avoided reading them because I didn't want to be reminded of the relationship. However, as I opened each card, I remembered the occasions when he gave me each card: our anniversaries, Christmas, Valentine's Day, and those all-important "just because" days. Surprisingly, I felt a great sense of freedom while remembering our reactions to each card. I found myself laughing at some of the more humorous ones and temporarily saddened by the "Baby, I'm sorry" cards.

Going through the cards allowed me to accept both the disappointment from the breakup and the breakup itself. I separate them because for a while I'd accepted one and not the other. Together they were too much emotionally for me to handle. Even when I saw his wife's picture in the paper, I was taken aback, but not taken back to the pain. It wasn't that I didn't care. I was moving on with my life and didn't want to take any pain or baggage from that season of my life into my future. The powerlessness I felt in losing my "man" to another woman no longer controlled me.

I spent a lot of time evaluating and reevaluating the relationship. I struggled to maintain a healthy balance between how the relationship actually was and the romantic ideal of how I wanted it to be. Sometimes all I could hear were his voice and his words, "Other than our first date, nothing in our relationship should've happened!" I replayed in my mind how I had asked him to repeat those words and then reminded him of the friendship and romance that we'd built and shared over eighteen months. In fact, we'd talked many times about how God had brought us together initially at a Christian singles event. I was the MC/host and he was the comedian performing on the show. Our first date was part of the show's plan to show healthy Christian dating. However, as I stood alone facing the end of the relationship, I was stung by pain and reeling in disbelief at how he was now twisting into evil the relationship that he'd said many times was so good.

There were days, especially early on in the breakup when I sat in solitude and replayed this particular conversation over and over. Strangely enough, I sometimes found myself agreeing with his statement and saying, "Maybe we shouldn't have dated." During this period when there was no communication between us, I began to understand how very differently my ex saw the relationship. Because of my own personal and spiritual weaknesses, I had allowed myself to become entangled in his manipulation and forgot that we both had chosen to be in relationship with each other because it was good for us at the time.

Believing that the relationship was either all bad or all good meant that I didn't have to face the unpleasant things I was learning about myself. I could negate the lessons by saying that they didn't matter, because where I learned them wasn't right in the first place. By denying the lessons, I was also denying that God was behind teaching me about myself and showing me where I needed to improve. The freedom came in acknowledging that God's divine purpose is greater than the pain of the hardest lessons of life. Focusing on truth and freedom gave me a new perspective on our relationship. Trusting in God brought me to a place where I could recognize and accept truth and enjoy the freedom that came from it as described in John 8:32: "And ye shall know the truth, and the truth shall make you free."

Even months after we'd broken up, I'd made the mistake of allowing my ex's "truth" about our relationship to affect me. By reading the cards, God revealed the truth that his hand was present in our relationship. I still struggled to trust God with my pain and hurt, but as I did so, he began to show me the importance of balanced truth. Leaning to my ex's understanding of the relationship kept me in an unhealthy state of denial. It may have been easier to accept the truth that the relationship shouldn't have happened because we were no longer friends or on speaking terms, but it was much healthier to do as Proverbs 3:5 says: " Trust in the Lord with all thine heart; and lean not unto thine own understanding."

> **RECOVERY TIP:**
> *Keep an open mind to the truth of the relationship just ended—it wasn't all good; it wasn't all bad. Believing so will keep you from truth and freedom.*

An influential and denied toxin in a love hangover is the feeling of powerlessness. Many adults spend time in relationships trying to untie the knots from our childhoods in which we were under- or overcontrolled by others. As adults we overcompensate to regain what we have lost when our parents, friends, siblings, or lovers reject us.

- Overcontrolling parents make us feel inadequate and shamed.
- Abandonment by our parents leaves us feeling powerless and with a great sense of loss.

Powerlessness emphasizes our inability to understand and ultimately control our emotions. The love hangover emphasizes our inability to control our circumstances. We can and must control our reaction to these circumstances.

I had so many emotions pulling and tugging at me that I didn't realize I was out of control until I made conscious attempts to regain it.

Powerlessness is such a destructive toxin—it has an octopus-like reach with tentacles that affect many areas of your life.

My relationship with God was most affected by this powerlessness. For the longest time, I thought that God was mad and disappointed in me. That must be why he allowed a man I truly loved to leave me and marry another woman.

> **RECOVERY TIP:**
>
> *Power comes in turning your heart to God and releasing the burdens of your heart. It forces you to deal with your inabilities and limitations.*

Believing that there was power in my prayer and in the prayers of others, I was embraced by a group of sister-friends who prayed for the relationship. The months of unanswered prayers for understanding and even my futile prayers for God to change my ex's heart were mind-numbing. I learned the painful but all-important lesson through the silence of unanswered prayers that all power belongs to God.

Power comes not in our prayers being answered but in turning our hearts to God and releasing the burdens of our hearts. It takes a great deal of trust to give our most secret emotional and spiritual burdens to God.

Turning to God forces us to deal with our inabilities and the limitations of our humanness. Only after we accept these limitations can we embrace the limitless power of God.

It was especially hard to deal with the feeling of powerlessness in having another woman essentially "take my man." She got him to do in seven months what he wouldn't do for me in eighteen months of dating. Was she smarter, better looking, or more spiritual than me? These questions tormented me for over a year after our relationship ended—he had emphatically stated over and over that she was just a "friend." Perhaps if I had put my foot down about their relationship while my ex and I were dating, he wouldn't have married her.

Does the fact that she now carries his name or will one day have his children make her a "better" woman? What did she do to persuade him to marry her? What did she do with his family that was better than what I did? Was she a better cook, better lover? These were questions that dominated my mind for months.

I immediately and destructively labeled her a whore. I didn't actually verbalize it, but I thought it enough. Not surprisingly, others had no problem saying it for me. I thought that I was being the mature Christian by not calling her names, but I soon realized that my criticism was a smoke screen for my fear that I was not woman enough. Despite losing weight and taking fairly good care of myself, I still was outmatched and outwitted by her.

By keeping myself in the "competition" mode for his love, even regrettably after the breakup, I didn't see that competition for love is not of God because it is rooted in pride and jealousy. Pride and jealousy are destructive aftereffects of years of powerlessness.

Then the light bulb came on: She may be married to the man I wanted to be with, but she only has the power that I give her in my negative thoughts, actions, and attitudes. Giving her control was crazy, unhealthy, and ungodly. This method of thinking kept me vulnerable and in a state of denial. It's not an issue of one being a better man or woman, it is about realizing that we are both valuable in God's eyes. There doesn't have to be an explanation of why she is now married to him.

True power comes in the ability to grow and accept the things that we can't change and embrace the truth of unexplainable circumstances. Acceptance, not understanding, is where we have the most power.

Post-Love Hangover Reflection

I DIDN'T REALIZE UNTIL MUCH LATER that I had read and destroyed the cards the day after they got married. It's as if we both officially let go of each other at the same time. How wonderful and awesome for God! Sometimes I wonder if I should have clipped out my ex's wife's picture. Not to throw darts at but as a reminder of the confidence that I had gained. A sign of my renewed trust in God and others, my greater appreciation for adversity, my increased thirst for righteousness and holiness. A measure of the peace with which I have boldly withstood storms, of the love I have developed for my enemies, and of my permanent song of praise for God's triumphs.

Chapter 9

Thinking Outside the Box

Today I had a conversation with the mother of my ex's godson. She seemed quite surprised when I told her that my ex-boyfriend and I no longer communicated. I thank God for divine protection and answered prayers. Months ago, I would have been consumed by fear and probably would not have been comfortable talking to her. Thank you, God, for healing. But by facing those old ghosts, I realize that where truth is, fears subside; where fear is, truth subsides.

I thank you, God, for today. I no longer feel the spirit of heaviness from my recent heartbreak. I believe that my hurt was caused not by loving him so much but by my not loving myself enough and refusing to allow you to love me. When I prayed yesterday in earnest for healing and restoration, I knew that you could do it—it's not about you taking so long, it's about me taking so long. When I said, "Okay, God," that's when it happened.

I NEVER THOUGHT I would get to the point of emotional healing soon enough. I knew it would happen, but it wasn't happening fast enough for me. I thought that I would always shudder uncomfortably whenever I heard his name. I remember during a conversation with the mother of my ex's godchild that she seemed to be picking for some kind of response because she made sure to mention the wedding. I'm so glad that I didn't have to stifle any feelings of rage or anger. They weren't there. I saw the conversation as a test and a chance to see just how much I'd grown. Unlike the past, there was no emotional backlash of tears after the conversation. My healing had finally come.

It was comforting being outside the "normal" dating world while I was with my ex, but I was now challenged with the possibility of dating again. I hadn't dated since the breakup and wasn't planning to do so any time soon. I knew that dating would mean thinking outside the box.

"Think outside the box." If you spent any time in corporate America in the 80s or 90s, you heard this term frequently. In some cases, this annoying phrase became an equally annoying mantra for self-appointed, self-help gurus. Put simply, it refers to changing the way you think about yourself, your things, and the situations in which you are placed.

Boxes, by themselves, are practical and necessary things that we often take for granted. They protect, shield, and cover our precious and not so precious belongings and keep them safe. Interestingly, boxes have the most use when we are in the process of moving, have moved, or plan to move. Boxes are used to transport our valuables so that they can maintain their original conditions.

You may be asking yourself, like I have many times, If boxes do all these great things, why should I think outside the box? A "box" can be a place of safety and comfort during and after an emotional heartbreak. These things are all very important to make sure you can move into future healthier relationships.

Unfortunately, "boxes" of comfort can also keep you in a place so familiar that your growth is ultimately hindered. Boxes provide boundaries and keep some things that you need out and prevent you from enjoying some things. In the case of a love hangover, boxes of sentimentality provide just the right tool to carry our emotional baggage from one relationship to another.

I had an interesting experience with my own boxes of memories recently when I went to my parents' home in San Antonio. While there, I had a chance to search through some boxes in their storage house. The boxes were full of pictures and papers, and held lots of memories. Most of the stuff I eventually decided I didn't want, like old magazines or records that were unsalvageable because of time and weather. The items that I did save—how priceless they are! I found a book of school attendance records and honor roll certificates. I also found boxes of favorite old music. I laughed at the memories of long-lost loves, and memories of the crazy things my friends and I had considered fun came back when I listened to those old songs. Funny thing, however, looking back in retrospect, some of those things weren't so fun after all, or so valuable.

When my father asked me why I kept all of that stuff, I could only think, *Because I needed it.* I didn't really know for what; it was just comforting to know that my stuff was still there, that and whenever I needed it, I could get to it. Eventually, I began the time-consuming but fun task of cleaning out those boxes, unsure of what I would find. The passing of time changed my perspective on those things that I once thought I couldn't live without. Reflecting on both the tangible and intangible things from my new position "outside the box" allowed me to honestly assess what was most important. It also gave me the opportunity to let go of some of the things that were no longer of use.

Rather than "thinking outside the box," maybe you should start cleaning out the box, taking what you want from inside the box and then throwing the box away. To do this, you have to deal with the uncertainties of both the past and the future. God deals with this same type of uncertainty with Joshua after the death of Moses and admonishes him in Joshua 1:9: "Be strong and courageous. Do not be terrified; do not be discouraged, for the LORD your God will be with you wherever you go."

> **RECOVERY TIP:**
> *Before you can think outside the box in the area of relationships, you need to clean out the box—what have you learned that will help you deal with past and future uncertainties?*

It takes courage to go through your emotional boxes with their past disappointments. Thinking outside the box means that you don't allow the fears of past mistakes to keep you from enjoying the promises of successful relationships in the future.

Maybe your boxes are places, people, and circumstances of emotional comfort into which you have settled that may not be the best for you, but are tolerable. The boxes for those of us recovering from a past failed relationship sometimes are boundaries that we create to protect us from future hurt. In the end, these same boundaries also keep us from enjoying the benefit of new and healthier relationships.

Post-Love Hangover Reflection

IT'S AMAZING HOW WE ARE KEPT IN BONDAGE by fear of things that never happen. The fear of saying something negative about my ex to others kept my emotional and spiritual wheels spinning. I was so distracted by a fear that I wasn't preparing adequately for the next season of my life. This was a nice little reminder that most of my love hangover was caused by both fear and anger: fear of letting go, and anger because I seemingly couldn't.

A few people have told me that they'll believe I'm over my ex when I get into a serious relationship again. For me, the best sign of healing is how I do when I am by myself. I'm now convinced that my emotional life will show "completion" because I am taking my healing with me into my next relationship—I do not expect it to just happen.

Whispers of Love

Pause for Reflection

From Me to You

Have you ever loved someone and wondered if they loved you?
Have you ever wished you could be with someone
and wondered if they wished it too?
Have you ever just dreamed of someone
that you knew was your destiny?
What's keeping you apart—is it air, distance, mileage, or all three?
Life is too short to let good things pass us by.
We don't want to say later I wish I had given it a try.
Tomorrow is not a guarantee, yesterday is gone.
The present is only here temporarily, it won't be here long.
The future is very bright if you're blessed to live past the night.
Loved ones are a treasure worth more than any amount of money.
Good friends are a jewel as sweet as any honey.
So, if you find someone who puts a sparkle in your eye,
someone who will be there for you if something makes you cry,
someone who will listen to you talk all night,
someone who will calm your fears if you experience fright,
someone who you truly know will always have your back,
someone who will give you a dollar
if that's all they have in their sack,

someone who will hold you all night long
after they massage your back and ask how your day had gone . . .

One day one of you will have to give
and take a chance to see if the love is truly real.
On the other hand, maybe not let life pass you by
and as you get older and years pass on
you'll say "I wish I had given it a try."

You may meet someone new and a relationship may start,
but one thing they will never have,
and that's your entire heart.
So, tell that special someone you love them
no matter how hard it seems.
Tell people you care about them even if they don't say anything.
People should take advantage of life
because it will definitely pass you by
And the next time a tear rolls down your face,
think of the friend you let pass.

Tracy A. Mayfield (© 2001)

Describe how being rejected affects you. Does it make you bitter or better?

Do not be deceived, God is not mocked;
for whatever a man sows, that he will also reap.

Galatians 6:7

Think of ways to make use of the times when you are unable to sleep. (prayer, etc.)

> *When you lie down, you will not be afraid;*
> *Yes, you will lie down and your sleep will be sweet.*
> Proverbs 3:24

Do you feel your ex betrayed you? Why or why not?

> *Let your conduct be without covetousness;*
> *be content with such things as you have.*
> *For He Himself has said, "I will never leave you nor forsake you."*
> Hebrews 13:5

How much did pride play in your actions after your breakup(s)?

> *Pride goes before destruction,*
> *And a haughty spirit before a fall.*
> *Better to be of a humble spirit with the lowly,*
> *Than to divide the spoil with the proud.*
> Proverbs 16:18–19

What are your three biggest regrets and three things valued most about the relationship?

> *And be kind to one another, tenderhearted,*
> *forgiving one another, even as God in Christ forgave you.*
> Ephesians 4:32

Have you forgiven your ex? Why or why not?

Part 4

LOVE

Through the LORD's mercies
we are not consumed,
Because his compassions fail not.
They are new every morning;
Great is Your faithfulness.

Lamentations 3:22–23

"THE MORE YOU BEGAN TO BE MEAN TO ME,
THE MORE I WAS LOSING CONTROL—
AND I HATED IT. I WASN'T ANGRY AT YOU
FOR PHONING LATER THAN YOU SAID YOU WOULD,
FOR ENDING AN EVENING EARLY BECAUSE YOU
WERE GENUINELY TIRED—I WAS ANGRY AT MYSELF
FOR ALLOWING IT TO MATTER THAT MUCH."

—*Gloria Naylor*

Love. A difficult topic to discuss. In recovering from a love hangover, we are entangled in the web of failed relationships where love sought was seemingly not found. Journaling can be an effective tool of self-discovery, and journaling about love can aid your development of a greater understanding of this action/emotion. Journal for at least one week on the subject of love. Here are some questions you might ask yourself to get started:

Day one: Write your personal definition of love and write down the questions you have about love.

Day two: Whom have I shown love to? (past and present) Who has shown love to me? (past and present)

Day three: What scenes in nature remind me of God's love?

Day four: What milestones in my life remind me of God's love for me?

Day five: How do I show myself that I love me?

Day six: When have I felt love failed me?

Day seven: Over the course of my life, what lessons in love have I learned?

> *"Forsake foolishness and live,*
> *And go in the way of understanding."*
>
> Proverbs 9:6

Chapter 10

Is It Love . . .
Or Are You a Bellywarmer?

I regretted many things about my relationship with my ex, but nothing more than the fact that we had premarital sex. I'm not so sure he believed me, but I meant it when I apologized to him after the breakup for having sex with him. I knew it was wrong, but for some reason, didn't have the self-control not to indulge. I wonder if we hadn't had sex, whether he would have married me? Even while we were dating, I knew that it was changing our relationship. I'd just fooled myself into believing that it was a good change.

B Y THE TIME I wrote this, I was at peace about the end of the relationship. My sleeping and eating patterns had returned to normal. I'd even been on a few out-of-town trips that gave me a much-needed break. I was not in a relationship or even thinking about one at this point, but I was now thinking about what I could do to avoid another shipwrecked relationship.

I thought back on my relationships with men that had been the most positive, both romantic and platonic. I realized that the relationships where there was no sex involved always ended with us remaining friends. The ones where sex was involved never did. As best I could see, the introduction of sex changed the potential for a mutually satisfying, mature, permanent friendship into an unbalanced, immature, and temporary one.

> **RECOVERY TIP:**
> *The introduction of sex into a relationship changes the potential for friendship—from mutually satisfying, mature, and permanent to unbalanced, immature, and temporary.*

The classic television miniseries *Roots* has a very compelling scene that takes place on one of the African slave-trading ships. In the scene, the captain of the ship indignantly refuses a very generous offer by one of his sailors for a "bellywarmer." The bellywarmer was one of the female African slaves who was used as temporary sexual satisfaction and a source of heat during the long and sometimes cold journey of the middle passage. The bellywarmer was always a temporary comfort for the long-term journey.

Many of us unwittingly enter into relationships with and become bellywarmers ourselves. We allow impatience and a lust for temporary pleasures to have greater control over us than godly patience and righteousness. Most relationships start off with a sincere desire to connect with someone else. Perhaps you'll see yourself in the following scenario:

Lately, I have been so at peace with myself; it is uncanny. My worries are no more. My burdens feather light. My bills will be paid in due time. No sweat. My enemies and fair-weather friends, who indeed abuse my kindness and generosity, I grant carte blanche. My tired boss and his tired wages and forever empty promises for promotion, I gladly accept with utmost gratitude and patience. What's wrong with me, you ask? You guessed it, "I'm hooked on love!"

Don't get me wrong. It wasn't your everyday boy-meets-girl storybook love—but close. Met her at the local record store. Fellas, she had serious presence. She had a certain *je ne sais quoi* about her. Her walk was effortlessly graceful, her demeanor mesmerizing. Her style undeniably unique: jazzy, sophisticated, with a touch of Cosmo all in one. Her confidence was magnetic: effervescent yet pleasantly attractive. Her complexion was flawless. She was potentially my queen and had jet-black, shoulder-length hair. Her almond-shaped eyes were as deep as the ocean waters; her sculpted body to the likes of Da Vinci or even Michelangelo. Her sexy voice, uttering even the simplest of words, was soft, yet soothing. She was a quiet storm.

Today was the release of the new Brian McKnight album. It was around ten til closing and the checkout line growing by the minute. I was already toward the end of the R&B section thumbing through CDs. Debonair by nature and suave by choice, I chose to play it cool. Or at least that was the plan: heart racing and palms perspiring, I began to have visions of us taking a midnight stroll along the beach holding hands. Horseback riding in San Bernadino Valley. Dining at the finest restaurants. . . . Then I heard, "Excuse me. Hello. Excuse me. Hello! May I please . . ." My sweaty hand rested on the last two Brian McKnight CDs.

Her voice broke me down like Jenga without even trying! Negative cool points indeed, but the soon-to-follow eye contact turned the butterflies in my stomach into doves of potential love and happiness… 'So I guess we have the last two copies of the new McKnight, huh?' she smiled. Tongue-tied and afraid to even dream of undressing her with my eyes, I stood struggling with my subject and verb agreement. She tactfully sensed my awe and questioned, "So, what's your name?"

"Phil, what's up?" I heard over my shoulder. "We are still on for the game tonight, right? Eight-thirty. Don't be late," as my friend Mike laid his hand on my shoulder in passing. "Nice, nice," he affirmed, with head nodding as he passed on by, turning to look back. Perfect timing, I thought. Just as I was all choked up, it was like he knocked the nerves out of me. Now I was cool. It was time to regroup. Our eyes met once again as she turned back from watching Mike pass. I said, "Phillip. My name is Phillip, but most call me Phil. And yours?"

"Thought you'd never ask. It's Cherie. Cherie Hightower," she smiled. We stood face to face. Nothing between our lips but air and opportunity, or should I say fire and desire.

A week later we did brunch. The next, a local play and dinner at Vargo's. Over the next couple months, every weekend brought more spontaneous excursions and adventures, one after another. Every weekday in between, intimate phone conversations and lunch whenever our schedules permitted. Four months later, Martha's Vineyard. We both loved to travel. She became my lifeline and

I became hers. My happiness now included her. I felt like I couldn't even appreciate it or experience it without her. I desired no independence from her. And it felt good!

I knew she would always be there for me and I for her. Besides, the woman is always ready to be by a man's side. It is usually the brother who isn't ready to settle down, chasing Wilt Chamberlain's legendary record. I have had my share of women. Our friends didn't understand. Especially my boys. They accused me of selling out and being soft "all in love." Well, I was in love and not ashamed to admit it, manhood still 100 percent intact, my boys still my boys. I had just come to a new stage in life. More mature and in tune with what I wanted. She was my Cherie amour, no doubt. I admit this was new to me. I mean, this girl was different. They thought we spent too much time together.

> RECOVERY TIP:
> *No relationship is perfect. Accept the fact that your ex-relationship wasn't perfect, and then it changed—it was never perfect from the beginning.*

Besides, what kind of friends wouldn't want to see us happy? We never had any major arguments. We were always understanding of each other, willing to make sacrifices. We were both so into each other. Her intimacies were mine. My secrets were now hers. We were everything to each other and that's all that mattered. It was the perfect relationship. Fail-proof. People envied what Cherie and I had.

We became so wrapped up in each other emotionally and sexually that we didn't see that we were headed for a collision between our desires and God's plan for the best. After our first sexual experience, which we both thought made things better, what had been playful, respectful arguments now became full-fledged, verbally intense fights. We finally had to admit that the relationship that we wanted to be life-lasting would not last past the end of the month. When it ended, we were both crushed and forced to deal with the reality of the "mourning after."

I see so much of my ex and our relationship in the above scenario. The mourning after forced me to look at myself and my ex and the relationship we had created. Once I stopped looking with romantic idealism at the relationship, I was able to be realistic about it. No relationship is perfect, because two imperfect people make up a relationship.

What struck me about my ex's perception was his statement that our relationship was at one point "perfect, then it changed." I remember thinking this was odd because we are imperfect people—the relationship could never have been perfect.

We did not honor God with our bodies, our talents, and our time. We spent entirely too much time by ourselves. Because we were so isolated, we easily fell into sexual immorality and became sexually intimate very early in the relationship. Now, granted, we struggled with keeping the relationship pure, but because this important boundary of intimacy was crossed, we also did things like spending the night with each other.

Our relationship did not begin to revolve around our sexuality, but it became a very distracting part. We made many attempts to stop, once going as long as two months without sex. However, we were always pulled back into the sexual intimacy. Near the end of the relationship, I shared with him that I wanted the relationship to give God glory and honor and wanted to stop having sex. I even told him excitedly a few weeks before we broke up that I was glad that our relationship had finally become the kind that God had wanted all along—we were no longer having sex. His response was a blank stare, and no verbal response.

I talked to others who had been sexually intimate before marriage—some even had lived together and eventually gotten married. I figured, why should our relationship have been any different?

Sex. It's amazing how this three-letter word can cause so many big problems in a relationship. For myself, the introduction of sexual intimacy seemed natural and harmless. We weren't planning for it to happen and because of the idea that we could handle advanced foreplay and heavy petting, we first got swept into a tide of justification and then disobedience. Our desire to satisfy each other became at times overwhelming. But the sex only satisfied surface and superficial desires. For my ex-boyfriend and me, we still had those issues and concerns after we stopped making love, but because we were sexually satisfied, we chose to ignore dealing with them and resolving them.

Tonight our love making was very passionate. I want to please him sexually and told him repeatedly. I realize after it was over that I didn't want to make love anymore. Once again, this is my struggle. Flesh and spirit. I wonder if we'll ever return to how it was when we first met and didn't have sex. He didn't respond when I talked about getting married and feeling guilty about having sex. I guess I feel like he doesn't respect me anymore. Oh, how I wish things would change.

THIS IS A JOURNAL ENTRY from about six months into our relationship. Rereading it years later, I recognize questions and doubts about the relationship and our future. I knew then that there was a problem, but refused to recognize the seriousness of it. It was easier to live in denial than confront the truth.

> RECOVERY TIP:
> *Sex does not equate with security—the sexual intimacy of a romantic premarital relationship may fool you into a counterfeit sense of safety.*

We both knew having sex was wrong and often talked about what we would do to stop. We even prayed together about it. However, I believe our immaturity and desire for intimacy, even counterfeit, overshadowed our judgment and ability to remain true to our vows of celibacy. How did this affect our relationship? We did not fully develop a godly foundation of friendship and companionship.

One soothing memory I have from my childhood is the comfort in knowing my father was either at home, on his way home, or a phone call away. There is still an indescribable and invaluable confidence I feel knowing that he is just a phone call or a short plane ride away. I find myself seeking this same type of security in my relationships with the opposite sex. I love and respect my father for providing for our family financially, emotionally, and spiritually.

I've come to look for this same type of comfort in my romantic relationships. Unfortunately, I've found counterfeit safety from sexually intimate, premarital relationships.

One of the things I regret most about my relationship is losing my feeling of safety. The safety came from knowing the person was willing to allow me to be my most intimate and naked. I marveled that he would still want me after seeing all the bumps and bruises, emotionally and spiritually.

With my ex, I remember melting into his arms and feeling so secure. In hindsight, I realize that this security was based on a counterfeit intimacy which breeds a false sense of security. Seven or eight months into our relationship, I struggled with feeling secure. Pressures from family and friends were taking a toll (or I thought they were) on our relationship. I was anxious and eager to restore the security that I felt I was losing.

I enjoyed the sexual intimacy because it fooled me into thinking that we were becoming closer. In fact, we were becoming more distant. Toward the end, I was so hungry for the warmth of security that I decided ending our sexual intimacy would lead to and foster the return of emotional intimacy. I was so very disappointed when this security didn't return. It seemed as though it all but evaporated when I told my ex that I didn't want to have sex again until we were married because I wanted our relationship to be in line with God's plan for our lives.

Needless to say, we never to got to where I think God wanted us. The damage done by sexual intimacy seemed too difficult to overcome.

Dr. Claudette Copeland describes how sexual intimacy can be seen as the delicate relationship between Kleenex and tape. The woman is the Kleenex and the man is the piece of invisible tape. When the act of sexual intimacy occurs, the tape attaches itself to the Kleenex. There's more of the Kleenex than there is of the tape. This implies that women have more to share and potentially lose when it comes to emotional and sexual intimacy.

The piece of tape by its nature is intended to attach to something. The act of sexual intimacy involves the woman opening a part or all of herself to the man. Contrary to popular belief, it is the man who initiates attachment and detachment. When women step into this role in the relationship, the balance of power and emotional control is upset. After each sexual encounter, the Kleenex and tape come apart, leaving less of the Kleenex and less "stickability" to the tape.

The aftermath of premarital sex causes the greatest damage. Because there is no spiritual covenant, there is a destructive tearing/ripping apart between both parties. What happens next is even more troubling. The woman loses a part of herself when the man detaches. She is left torn and damaged, with significant pieces of her emotional and sexual self gone. It's not until the woman attempts to reconnect with another man that the void and damage is recognized.

What occurs to the man is equally significant. The man may leave the relationship and detach himself still intact, but he then takes a part of the woman with him. It is only when he attempts to attach himself to another woman that he realizes that his "stickability" is diminished. Enough serial monogamous relationships leave him ultimately unable to attach in a healthy way to any woman. Bits and pieces of his previous relationships prevent any real emotional, physical, and spiritual intimacy.

There is safety in the initial attachment, but in the end, after the sexual contact, the safety that the woman desires is never completely fulfilled. Premature sex leads to an unbreachable void. All too often, women spend the remainder of their relationship and lives attempting to replace the lost safety with things like material possessions or unsafe people.

Continued sexual activity will not restore this lost feeling of safety. It can only be restored by the one who gives true safety. The return of purity and safety comes in the return to truth and the truth of the relationship, which only comes through a real relationship with Jesus Christ. Sexual intimacy builds a deceptive cloud that makes the truth about safety fuzzy. I was just "having fun" and "kickin' it" are rationalizations and cover up the sad realization that safety is gone.

Post-Love Hangover Reflection

I REALIZE NOW THAT PART of the "thrill" of being in a relationship is balanced by the compromises you make to remain in that relationship. Unfortunately, I made the mistake of being too willing to compromise to remain with my ex. In the end, I was left more devastated because not only had I lost him, I'd also lost my strength of character—I chose not to tell him how I really felt about some very important things, including sexuality. I sacrificed building character because I thought I was building a relationship.

> RECOVERY TIP:
> *The thrill of being in a relationship is balanced by compromises you have to make—don't be willing to sacrifice character for the relationship.*

Now I know that not being swayed by the opinions of others builds strength of character. People who always worry about what others think place themselves in a position of being manipulated. It takes a great inner strength to not allow others to change you. It also requires placing and reinforcing the proper relationship boundaries—in other words, knowing when and how to say no. Especially when it comes to sex. It also means being comfortable in saying no to others without being controlled by their emotions.

Often we allow the emotions of others to affect our integrity; we don't want to hurt someone's feelings so we tell a little (or even a big) lie to save their feelings. In the end we lose a part of our integrity. People might accuse you of being selfish and uncaring when it comes to their feelings. But in reality, your integrity will have a bigger impact on how you live your life. Ask yourself: Is saving someone else's feelings worth losing your integrity?

Trusting the Lord, as the Scripture states, will open the door for you to receive many blessings. One of the greatest of these is the peace of mind that comes from knowing you've maintained your integrity.

Chapter 11

Brother to Sister . . .
Sister to Brother

It's been almost a year since the breakup and I feel pretty good. I can tell that I'm closer to complete healing because I'm entertaining the thought of casually dating again. My job allows me to meet a variety of men, which also gives me a chance to test out my newly found wholeness. I am not looking to get married to any of them. I'm just interested in finding someone who'll be a safe companion to the many social events my job sends me to. I'm perfectly content to go by myself, but I think I need to start inviting others into my space. The only problem is when I go to these social events, I have to deal with people asking me questions about my ex and our relationship. This is when I wish he were here and not living in another city so he could answer their questions.

BY THIS POINT, I'd been able to see much growth in both my spiritual and emotional life. I was now looking at things much more clearly. And, best of all, I had conquered my fear of social engagements. I was going to banquets, concerts, movies, etc., when just a few months before, I was only going to work and back. It amazed me how much I'd changed from being such a hermit and so antisocial. I guess facing the fear of people rejecting me gave me confidence.

In going to social events, I also had to face the fear of someone asking me about my ex. It hadn't been a year since we'd broken up and people still asked when we were getting married. I was now able to tell them what happened without having an extreme emotional backlash. However, I was forced to deal with another question for God. Why did you let him move away and leave me here to answer the questions about our relationship? I really didn't think it was fair that I was the one wronged, but now I had to respond with a polite smile that we were no longer dating.

> **RECOVERY TIP:**
> *Facing the fear of rejection will give you confidence—you will be able to face people and tell them what happened without experiencing an extreme emotional backlash.*

A young girl, prim and proper, loses her virginity before marriage and she embarks on a potentially destructive life of promiscuity. A young male, same age and with the same sense of innocence, loses his virginity, and he enters manhood. Sexist? Chauvinistic? Maybe. Reality? Indeed. Throughout history, masculinity and sexual expression have enjoyed normal connotations. There are no rules. No governing societal pressure to discourage young men from experiencing premarital, consensual sex. This is greatly due to societal norms that have been passed down from generation to generation.

Why does this double standard exist? Why does the girl have to wear "the scarlet letter" and the guy gets to be "the mack"? This is not something that suddenly manifests itself in years of early puberty. It starts much earlier in child development.

A growing boy often conveys his inner feelings, desires, and dislikes through physical expression. If he feels like punching, he should punch! Kicking, he should kick! Climbing, he should climb! Running, he should run! Crying, however, he should not cry. Big boys don't cry!

But if she wants to cry, hand her a box of Kleenex. If she feels like punching, she better not! Kicking, she should redirect that energy into combing Barbie's hair. Climbing, she better think of how unlady-like that would be and how disappointed her parents would be. If a man feels threatened, he protects, defends, and even sometimes destroys. Think of the many contact sports that exist today. Boxing, wrestling, martial arts, ice hockey, football, soccer, just to name a few. Despite the million-dollar contracts and signing bonuses, many of these brutes would do it just for the pleasure.

The sport of sexual pleasure, just as the others, is one of physical expression. A rough day at the steel mill or a hectic day at the office versus a stress-free, unexpectedly shortened four-hour workday at the firm determines whether there will be some "making love" or some "manhandling rough sex" going on that night. Seek, prey, and conquer is the point here. Young girls later maturing to women are taught to repress their most primitive emotions and feelings that are not acceptable socially. They develop a more internally based sense of basic emotional response, one that is less often acquired by their male counterpart. Maybe this further supports why it is not so common to meet a "sensitive man," one who is in touch with his emotions and manhood at the same time and unafraid to reveal such.

What Men Really Want and How
Sex Affects Their View of Relationships

For the man, who as a boy was taught to manifest every emotion imaginable through physical expression, sex is an external experience. A man uses sex as a method of expression. He communicates his passion through acting out his lust and desire as well as his love. Sex to a man is an act where he releases a part of him. Ultimate pleasure, peace, and tranquility soon follow this release. His once rapid heartbeat returns to normal. Beads of sweat rolling down his back and dripping from the tip of his nose onto her body signify hard work and will soon evaporate into the atmosphere.

This is not to say that the sexual experience is not a soul-touching one for the man, but that the act is an external one. The soul is considered an "internal entity." So for a man to experience sex as a soul-touching one, it can be logically argued that he must choose whether to allow passionate love-making to touch his soul!

Maybe there is some truth in the saying "Men can separate sex and love. Woman can't." If so, maybe this is not by choice. Maybe it is predicated by our basic biological expression of our sexuality. Most men know whether they desire sexual relations with a woman the moment they lay eyes on her. Men interpret her body language, how well-kept she is, her dress, her style, and her sensuality or lack thereof. Nonverbal communication is the core of comfortableness. We are always communicating with our body language. So the initial question is whether she is purposefully using her body as a form of communication despite whatever small talk is being exchanged simultaneously. The key here is the word "purposefully." Prolonged eye contact, casual touch, excessive and often undue laughter supported with a pleasant smile, sense of fondness, and, most importantly, body distance. Is she allowing me in her space? Or has she set obvious boundaries? These are some intangibles men may use to determine a woman's initial interest. Whether it is intimate or merely platonic? No matter how subtle her "body talk" may be, men are not apt to miss a single innuendo.

Some men wait until they get a sense of interest before they move to the next step of categorization. Basically men place women in three categories from a sexual viewpoint after their initial encounter: (1) lustful leisure, (2) sexual symbiosis, and (3) marriage material.

Lustful leisure: One-time offer. No guarantee. Driven by self-pleasure, curiosity, and lust. Emotional attachment is *not* an option.

Sexual symbiosis: Initially driven by self-pleasure, curiosity, and lust, as in lustful leisure. However, a "relationship" in the literal sense is established. The intimate interaction is mutually ongoing. It is recurrent and periodically longed for by both individuals. Attachment *is* an option. The indefinite nature of sexual symbiosis can be problematic. This category is the most dangerous of the three. There are no rules to when the "relationship" is terminated. It is like literally "walking blind in the middle of the road." No warning is promised. No caution. No detour. No yield sign. The ending is often devastating.

> RECOVERY TIP:
> *Be aware of your body language. You are always communicating with your body—and the message you are sending may not be as subtle as you think.*

Marriage material: Meets majority of "the standards." Can meet the parents. Includes those things that are most important to "him." May include: God-fearing. Trustworthy. Faithful. Supportive, offering constructive criticism yet understanding "the struggle." She is dependable. Educated. Caring. Generous. Classy. Submissive yet ambitious, respectable yet sensual, sophisticated yet sexy. Next to perfection in his eyes. She is his queen. His precious jewel. Priceless. Her unconditional love for him is as long and deep as the river Nile.

If the man feels the woman doesn't fit into either of these categories then either the man is not physically attracted to her, sees
her as the she's-like-a-sister-to-me-type, or the risk of embarking
on an intimate relationship does not outweigh the benefit.
Conversation often sheds light. It may further affirm or discourage
his desire to pursue his interests. Maybe he sees early signs of
emotional instability, baggage from a previous relationship, personality clash, or maybe her breath just stinks! It may also lead him to
recategorize her from "marriage material" to "lustful leisure" or
vice versa. Her past, if and when discussed, may be grounds for
recategorization. Promiscuity and past infidelity are the most
common reasons for such. No matter how many partners a man
has experienced in his time, she rarely can carry a similar record.

It is much harder for a woman to be upgraded than down-
graded. Being in a particular category sets the stage for the entire
dynamics of the intimate relationship.

What Women Really Want and How Sex Affects Their View of Relationships

Women want the following from relationships:

1. Safety that gives the secure foundation and a return to her
   childhood dream, or reality, of having a protective father.
2. A man working, which means he has a job, but also
   refers to a man who recognizes his purpose and is willing
   to help a woman recognize and pursue hers. Includes
   educational, spiritual, financial, and professional goals. He
   will have a vision for his life . . . not to impress her but to
   express himself. He will be mature enough to allow his
   vision for his life to become a part of her vision for her life
   and vice versa.

3. A man with potential: Women are nurturers and usually are willing to plant seeds and watch them grow. This is where women have the most difficult time. Because we like to nurture, we often don't like or realize when our time of planting seeds and harvesting has ended. We want to take credit for nurturing and harvesting a seed when it may be that our only purpose was to plant the seed. Someone else is supposed to watch it grow then maybe another enjoy the harvest. Each stage is equally important.

4. A man who wants to be friends as well as loved as a brother or counselor: Interestingly, with the right amount of time and effort, this category can become a friend with potential. Unlike some men, most women want the man whom they are sexually active with to be their friend.

5. A man who is giving: Is a generous person and willing to give to others. Women want to see that the man has enough emotional, financial, spiritual, and professional resolve to give to others and still take care of his home.

Just as men immediately size up women, women label and categorize just as quickly. Women use the same categories with one difference: Women are much more compassionate and forgiving when a man tries to transition out of one category. A woman's desire for emotional attachment makes her more forgiving and willing to watch the man grow like a garden. She may see the weeds, but she will also see the beauty of the grass and plants that surround it.

Two people in love. Souls intertwined. Scheduling and rescheduling. Prioritizing and reprioritizing to make more "quality time" for your newfound love. Midweek late-night phone conversations in the dark. Fighting sleep just to massage one another with "the vocab." Symbolic? "Love blind"? Perhaps. Love is a mystical magnetism that leaves our souls vulnerable to the unexpected? Definitely. Magical innuendoes teasing one another with endless possibilities. Strolls through the park followed by romantic candlelight dinners. Not played out. Just part of the "before play." Before what, you ask? Before the assurance of a successful pursuit.

> **RECOVERY TIP:**
> *Women and men both label and categorize each other, but women tend to be more compassionate and forgiving because of their emotional attachment.*

This is not to suggest that sex is all the man pursues. The decision for the woman to have premarital sex with a man may in a sense represent submissiveness and surrender. Giving in to her loins despite how she was taught as a young teenage girl to fear the very thought of such an act.

The anticipation surrounding sex is preoccupying, curiosity-driven, and overwhelming, all at the same time. Up until this point in the relationship everything had been so picture-perfect. Now the two of you are faced with, "Will he please me?" "Will I satisfy him?" "What if we don't connect physically as they have intellectually, emotionally, and spiritually?"

Sheer magnetism continues to draw your souls closer to being one. The next step is actual oneness—in the most literal sense. When the time is right, we feel it destined to happen. In the heat of "before play," our minds are already made up. "This is it. I would be crazy not to do this!" Desire mounts anxiety. Anxiety mounts even more desire. In the midst of these two come pure lust and curiosity which further mount both anxiety and desire. Morals and spiritual convictions, not purposely but conveniently, are thrown out the window. After all, rationale plays no role in "falling in love." Society doesn't teach us to rationalize our heartfelt emotions and decision making when dealing with this crazy thing called love. We just do it! Wisdom, understanding, and all that stuff come later, right? And usually after things don't work out and someone's heart is broken. . . .

Then it happens.

Our souls connect. We desire more. And we oblige each other. The next plateau and the next question is, "Who will be the first to say, 'I love you?' "

The act of "falling in love" is desired by many but experienced by few. Society suggests that this is the greatest feeling ever. To love and for that same love to be reciprocated simply defies words. "Falling in love." Such a sweet phrase.

Falling in love. *Falling in*. . . . Can you imagine any other scenario where "to fall" is actually desired? Falling usually precedes injury. Followed by disappointment, disgust, being distraught, discontentment, and distress. Many descriptive terms used when dealing with the mourning after. So, why would anyone want to fall?

Whether falling in love or falling in lust, both leave us vulnerable. Anytime you become dependent on someone else emotionally, yearning for their love, their affection, their time, their attention, and those late-night massages, you have just inherited the potential of being heartbroken. Just as your mate made the decision to love you, she can make the same decision to no longer love you. To no longer sleep with you. To no longer return your many phone calls. And even maybe leave you for a new love!

Just as falling in the literal sense leaves your destiny in the hands of gravity, "falling in love" leaves you in the capricious hands of your mate.

When dealing with the hurt and disappointment of a failed relationship, we often begin by trying to understand where or how things went wrong. We either blame ourselves or the other person, or even at times attempt to find a scapegoat—some circumstance beyond our control, irreconcilable differences, or conflict of interests—to be the reason to explain the breakup. Nonetheless, the mourning after still rears its ugly face with the reality that life must go on without that once-believed-to-be soulmate. The pain and confusion you are dealing with urges you to seek almost immediate understanding. Having an answer, no matter how lame or incredulous it may be, initially gives a temporary sense of comfort, allowing you to repress those feelings of sadness and abandonment. The key is to begin with self-searching, not self-blaming. Searching within yourself helps in several ways.

> **RECOVERY TIP:**
> *Only you can decide if you're falling in love or falling in lust—either way you are vulnerable because "falling" leaves your fate in the hands of your mate.*

Self-searching helps you make the necessary adjustments to avoid repeating mistakes when seeking "Mr. or Mrs. Right." After three years of seriously dating someone in a "time-out-for-games" period in your life, you are now distraught. What you are feeling is totally acceptable. You should begin by asking yourself, "What is it about him/her I miss that leaves me feeling so empty?" Intimacy? Companionship? Friendship? A sense of completeness? The first three, of course, can be remedied with time and a more worthy and mature partner. The fourth, the sense of completeness, makes you the most vulnerable for future disappointing relationships, especially if your mate is with you for some other reason.

As cliché as it may sound, it is without a doubt true that a companion should complement you, not complete you. When that "can't live without him/her" bug bites, it's like a self-consuming virus inside of you that unknowingly grows each day. Your dependency on that individual and false sense of never-ending security feeds it and may ultimately lead to the heartache of another failed relationship.

Someone asked me whether they should meet with their ex-boyfriend for dinner three months after their breakup. My response was simple: You were the dedicated, trustworthy, dependable caregiver of the two in the relationship. He was the questionably "honest," less-than-perfect, with-much-room-for-improvement boyfriend. His leaving appears to have been quite an unpleasant surprise. When two individuals in a serious relationship are "on the same page," equally valuing honesty and communication, very little should come as a surprise. Not being honest with your mate often precedes unwarranted vulnerability.

> **RECOVERY TIP:**
> *A companion should complement you, not complete you—that "can't live without him/her" dependency gives you a false sense of security and may lead to heartbreak.*

If you are having second thoughts about meeting with him and wonder what exactly he wants to "catch up" on, then you probably should listen to yourself. Intuition is a powerful intangible. Whether or not you had the chance to have closure, to answer all the whys, whats, and hows is not important. The truth is, you are still in a vulnerable state, wounded and heartbroken by his abandoning you. You can unknowingly prolong your hangover by believing that having some sort of answer is better than no answer, that it would lessen the frustration and confusion, no matter how illogical or absurd the reason. History is the past and the present can never match it exactly as it was. In your case, this is not what you desire anyway. Closing this chapter of your life will be the best decision to make.

Post-Love Hangover Reflection

IN WALKING THE AWKWARD STEPS of emotional recovery, one question comes up quite often. It's not "Why did this happen to me?" nor is it, "Have you seem him/her lately?" It's really very simply stated and much more complicated to answer: "How much more does God have to show you?" What more about the person

> RECOVERY TIP:
> *Getting over your love hangover will be easier after you honestly reassess what you wanted from the relationship—and you realize your ex couldn't give it to you.*

that you wish you were dating or may be dating does God have to show you before you realize and accept that it's probably not his best for you? After I honestly reassessed what I wanted in a relationship, and realized that my ex couldn't give it to me, it became much easier to accept that it was for the best that we were no longer together. I stopped seeing our breakup as punishment from God. I see it now as a sign of God's protection of my emotions. God had shown me clearly that my ex wasn't willing or able to provide the safety, security, trust, and loyalty that I desire.

I matured enough to accept this reality, but I still found myself dealing with the same types of people from my past. I had to be careful not to allow what was comfortable and comforting to lull me back into emotional and spiritual bondage. I had to pray for God to fill those "empty" spaces with his love, peace, grace, and mercy. It was only then that I became strong enough to be an effective witness to those who were hurting and seeking a safe sanctuary for truth with the hope that they would eventually be healed like me.

Whispers of Love

Pause for Reflection

Love Hangover: The Song

There were days when I thought about you.
There were days when I looked for you.
There were days when I called your name.
But you didn't answer, you never came.
So I took a step back then I realized, you weren't the one
to be in my life. So, now I need God to help me get through.
(you see) I've got a love hangover, and it's because of you!

There were days when I thought about you.
There were days when I looked for you.
There were days when I called your name.
But you never answered, you never came.
But when you took a step back and realized that I am the one
you need in your life. Then you cried out to me to help you get through.
See, I am love hanging over, and it's all about you!!!

God, I can't believe that you would do this to me!
Child, if I hadn't been there, you would never be free!
But, Lord, why? Why would you do it this way?
Child, I needed you for this time and this day!

© 2001 Dormel Cobbs-Thompson

Have you learned to be content with not being in a relationship? Why or why not?

Now godliness with contentment is great gain.
For we brought nothing into this world,
and it is certain we can carry nothing out.
1 Timothy 6:6–7

What have you felt guilty about after your breakup? Do you feel like God has eased that burden?

If we confess our sins, He is faithful and just
to forgive us our sins and to cleanse us
from all unrighteousness.
1 John 1:9

How did the breakup affect your intimacy with God and others? What steps have you taken or will you take to restore intimacy?

"As for you, my son Solomon, know the God of your father,
and serve Him with a loyal heart and with a willing mind;
for the LORD searches all hearts
and understands all the intent of the thoughts.
If you seek Him, He will be found by you;
but if you forsake Him, He will cast you off forever.
1 Chronicles 28:9

What are your one-year, five-year, ten-year spiritual and emotional plans for your life?

> *To everything there is a season,*
> *A time for every purpose under heaven.*
> Ecclesiastes 3:1

What's the best and worst thing you've learned about yourself since the breakup?

> *For I know the thoughts that I think toward you, says the LORD,*
> *thoughts of peace and not of evil, to give you a future and a hope.*
> Jeremiah 29:11

Did the relationship help fulfill God's purpose for your life?

Part 5

JOY

*For his anger
is but for a moment,
His favour is for life,
Weeping may endure for a night,
But joy comes in the morning.*

Psalm 30:5

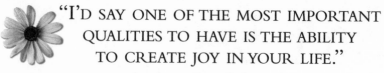

"I'D SAY ONE OF THE MOST IMPORTANT QUALITIES TO HAVE IS THE ABILITY TO CREATE JOY IN YOUR LIFE."

—*Bessie Delany*

While reading this book on recovering from a love hangover, it can be tempting to believe that after you have recovered, you will once again experience joy. Don't wait. Begin now to act as if you are in that place of joy. Tomorrow is not promised.

Tips on creating joy in your life:

- Seek salvation through Jesus Christ.
- Spend more time with people who inspire and motivate you than with people who sap your energy and deplete you
- Lower your tolerance for things that drain you emotionally. Limit your exposure to negativity.
- Monitor your calendar. Make sure that you are spending time with loved ones, doing your favorite hobby, remembering birthdays and anniversaries with at least a phone call or note.

Then he said to them, "Go your way, eat the fat, and drink the sweet, and send portions to those for whom nothing is prepared; for this day is holy unto our LORD. Do not sorrow, for the joy of the LORD is your strength."

Nehemiah 8:10

Chapter 12

Breaking Soul Ties

I'm so thankful to God that he protected me after our relationship ended. I prided myself on not calling my ex back and asking for one more chance. I hear people talk a lot about taking their ex back. I also wonder why. It seemed great to me to be friends with an "ex," but I thought it would be much healthier in the long run to have a clean break, no questions asked. The pain may still be there, but at least you don't have to see that person all the time. Sometimes, I'm a little lonesome, but I figure this is just a season I'm going through.

I will both lie down in peace, and sleep; For You alone,
O LORD, make me dwell in safety."

Psalm 4:8

WE SHALL OVERCOME SOMEDAY!" are words that I heard often during Black History Month at the many programs in churches and community centers about the achievements of African Americans. I'd also like to think it's because an ever-growing chorus of singles are happy that the relationship Bermuda Quadrangle (Thanksgiving, Christmas, New Year's, and Valentine's Day) is over. It's not that those who are unattached are jealous of people in relationships during that time of the year. It's because the focus of well-meaning friends, family members, and coworkers will shift from their usual stares of pity and, in some cases, taunts of ridicule because we didn't receive or give anything for one of these special holidays.

At this time of year, the empty side of your bed appears to grow bigger and the ache in your heart for someone special grows more powerful and painful. If you are brave enough to voice your feelings, you might get the following response: "Well, just find a boyfriend/girlfriend," or other words of "wisdom."

A friend sent me this poem to encourage me during a particularly lonely time. He told me that he didn't want to offer empty words or catch phrases, but wrote it one night when he himself was struggling with the emptiness of his bed and the loneliness in his heart. He hoped that reading the poem would help me develop a new perspective on what I saw as a deficit in my love life. Rather than see his life as empty because he wasn't in a relationship, he chose to see it as full of virtue.

To Sleep With Virtue

She held me just so,
Touched me right there,
And whispered her truths.

She heard my thoughts,
My words she spoke,
Made them ours.

To me she came on this
uneasiest of nights,
and together we slept.

Yes, I slept with virtue
Sweet, precious virtue,
My virtue.

© 2001 Wayne L. Tillman

> **RECOVERY TIP:**
> *Celebrate your*
> *singleness. Focus on*
> *the blessings of*
> *being successfully*
> *single rather than*
> *on the loneliness of*
> *being alone or on*
> *envying those who*
> *are married.*

I read and reread his poem after he sent it to me. His words of "change your perspective" from one of our conversations kept replaying in my mind. Even when I protested that it was so hard, he gently told me that he understood—that's why he wrote the poem.

Change how you see your current season of singleness as a time to spend woefully lonely and looking with envy at those who are married or otherwise attached. Just as it is a blessing to be with someone, it is a blessing to be successfully single.

Many of us waste our most productive years as singles focused on the emptiness of our beds and the "tragedy" of sleeping by ourselves rather than on the fullness and joy that comes from sleeping with our virtue.

> *"The thief does not come except to steal,*
> *and to kill, and to destroy.*
> *I have come that they may have life,*
> *and that they may have it more abundantly."* John 10:10

A few years ago, the movie *Sleeping with the Enemy* told a very frightening story of a woman who was mentally, physically, and verbally abused by her husband. Even though he tried to present himself as a loving spouse, in reality he was a vicious and vindictive man. Moviegoers seemed to connect with the theme that we are sometimes in relationships with people who present themselves as safe but, in truth, they often are seeking to destroy rather than protect us.

We can also sleep with the enemy, much like we sleep with our virtue. And like the movie, for some of us the enemy is an actual, physical person whom we no longer feel safe or comfortable around. I think for many more of us, however, the enemy is not an actual, physical person, but it is the words, actions, attitudes, and destructive pattern of behavior that keep us separated from or unwilling to accept the love of God in our lives. These thoughts are the whispers of the enemy (devil, Satan) that are intended to keep us from enjoying the fruitful lives that God has promised.

Unresolved disappointments are the seed for a harvest of bitterness, rooted in the attitude that you have the right to be mad at God because he didn't give you what you wanted. "My baby's daddy left me." "I didn't get the job I wanted." "I prayed and my mama still died." "I prayed and the thing that I was praying against still happened." These are just a few examples. It's perfectly okay to allow yourself to feel the frustration of disappointment, but it is important that we don't get enveloped in the entitlement of disappointment. It's so easy for us to allow that attitude to become our companion after we enter a season of unanswered prayers. God wants us to bring our disappointments to him. However, some of us bring the arrogance of the entitlement of unanswered prayers which we believe gives us the right to remain distant from God.

Speaking from my own personal experience, I know what it feels like to be angry at God because my prayers weren't answered. I even remember telling God, while in prayer, that I didn't see the need for prayer because it didn't work. I remember thinking, "What's the point in praying when you still don't get what you want? I could have spent my time watching TV and eating what I wanted as opposed to wasting time in prayer and fasting. What's the point?!" After my tirade, I was amazed by the fact that the floor didn't swallow me up with all my earthly possessions. I remember feeling relieved that I was still there, but also relieved that I had those feelings that I'd allowed to rock me to sleep at night and remain with me in the morning.

> **RECOVERY TIP:**
> *Not all prayers get answered. Prayer is not a selfish enterprise; it's not about getting things—it's about building a stronger relationship with God.*

Disappointment from unanswered prayer is the enemy because it fools you into believing that God is not listening and doesn't love you. God, like any loving father, just wants us to talk to him . . . in prayer. Prayer is not about getting an answer that we like, but it is about building a stronger relationship with God. Needless to say, I felt like I'd insulted God. I'd selfishly focused on getting the things that I knew God could give me rather than developing a relationship with God.

To some, that's not a great revelation—just a Sunday school lesson. I'd heard it before, but this time it made sense and surprisingly gave me comfort and peace in knowing that though I felt I'd lost so many things as a result of unanswered prayer, I was now a "winner" because I had a more intimate relationship with God. The best way to build intimacy is to increase communication. The most intimate thing you can do with someone is pray. If we want to increase our intimacy with God, we have to increase our communication . . . in other words, pray.

I can personally testify that once you start to spend time with God in prayer, it doesn't matter whether you get the "thing" that you want. All that matters is that you build a strong relationship with God.

A friend gave me this prayer to pray as I was struggling to break the soul ties to my ex. After praying it a few times, I noticed that my attitude toward him and our sexual intimacy changed. I no longer yearned for his touch. In fact, I was moved more to tears of repentance when I realized how much we'd hurt God by our disobedience. And for that, we both needed to ask for forgiveness.

A Prayer of Cleansing and
Breaking the Chains of Soul Ties

Dear Heavenly Father:

I come to you in the name of Jesus. I ask that you
 forgive me of all of my sins.
Please forgive me of all of the things I have done which
 were not pleasing in your sight
and which were contrary to your word and will for
 . my life.

I submit all of my soul, my body, my desires, and my
 emotions to you.
I denounce any conscious or subconscious attachments
 formed in my past:
past involvements, past emotional attachments,
and past premarital sexual relationships.

I denounce the emotional, physical, and spiritual ties
 formed by my involvement
in any forbidden sexual, mental, or emotional intimacy

outside of marriage and your will for my life.

I confess all of my ungodly spirit, soul, and body ties as
sin and I repent of them all.

I loose myself from all soul ties to past sexual partners
and ungodly relationships.

Please uproot all connections through sexual bondage,
emotional longings,

dependencies, frequent thoughts, fantasies, and enslaving
thoughts.

I bind every evil spirit that reinforced the soul ties and
any evil transference into my life

through ungodly associations in the name of Jesus.

I surrender my mind to Christ Jesus, so that I may have
the mind of Christ at all times.

I thank you, Lord, that I am being renewed and cleansed
in my mind.

Christ is transforming a work in me.

Lord, you said in your word that whatsoever things are
lovely, pure, honest, and of good report,

I should think on these things.

Help me to do that now in Jesus' name.

Lord, I ask you to cleanse my soul and to erase totally
from my memory bank

all illicit unions that I participated in.

Set me free so that I may serve only the purposes of God
and my mate.

Set me free from the bondage of guilt, anger, bitterness,
and revenge.

Let the blood of Christ Jesus purge me now in Jesus' name.

Father, now that I have asked you this and it is in accordance with your will for my life,

I believe I am totally forgiven and set free.

I recommit myself to you.

I thank you for a clean slate and a new lease on life in Jesus' name.

Amen.

© 2001 Rev. Karen C. Gaines

> **RECOVERY TIP:**
> *The lure toward destructive relationships is always there. Replace the emptiness of your love hangover with the fruit of the Spirit through prayer, consecration, and worship.*

But the fruit of the Spirit is love, joy, peace, longsuffering, kindness, goodness, faithfulness, gentleness, self-control."

Galatians 5:22

Sometimes, despite our best efforts, we are easily lured back into destructive relationships after God has shown us truth, delivered us out of bad relationships, and cleansed us spiritually and emotionally. Matthew 12:43–45 describes how the unclean spirit returns to the now cleaned house with seven other spirits that wreak havoc and greater devastation. Sometimes this happens because we allow ourselves to entertain familiar and comfortable spirits—people who are mysteriously drawn to us and to whom we find ourselves attracted.

A reason for this frustrating cycle is the lack of spiritual focus that sometimes occurs after a relationship ends. Rather than using that time to focus and renew our relationship with God, we choose to focus on our feelings of emptiness. In all honesty, that emptiness you feel once a relationship ends is not always a bad thing. It's a sign that God wants to fill you with the fruit of the Spirit that comes from spending quality time in prayer, consecration, and praise/worship.

Galatians 5:22 lists nine fruits of the spirit that come from embracing the Holy Spirit and submitting our lives to his guidance and direction. This spiritual fruit is the result of the seeds of obedience. Ironically, the nine fruits are greater than the eight spirits that try to occupy our cleaned spiritual house. When you have the harvest of all the fruits, you can effectively resist the attempted "home invasion" by the unclean spirits.

> **RECOVERY TIP:** *Decide for yourself to allow the Spirit of God to have control of your life—the result will be a great harvest that will fill your empty spaces and make you complete.*

Once you decide to allow the Spirit of God to have control of your life, the result will be a great harvest of these fruits which will fill those empty spaces and make you complete. When you enjoy life and relationships as a complete person, you will be able to resist the temptation to fill your life with people and relationships that are unhealthy.

The key to planting the seeds of the fruits of the Spirit is obedience . . . the key to harvesting the fruit is changing your behavior and meditating on God's word, like those listed below, as you continue the work of filling your empty spaces.

Love: *Beloved, let us love one another, for love is of God; and everyone who loves is born of God and knows God. He who does not love does not know God, for God is love.*
1 John 4:7, 8

Joy: *Do not sorrow, for the joy of the LORD is your strength.*
Nehemiah 8:10b

Peace: *You will keep him in perfect peace, Whose mind is stayed on You, Because he trusts in you.* Isaiah 26:3

Longsuffering: *The LORD is good to those who wait for Him, To the soul who seeks Him.* Lamentations 3:25

Kindness: *And be kind to one another, tenderhearted, forgiving one another, even as God in Christ forgave you.* Ephesians 4:32

Goodness: *Behold, I long for your precepts; Revive me in your righteousness.* Psalm 119:40

Faithfulness: *But the Lord is faithful, who will establish you and guard you from the evil one.* 2 Thessalonians 3:3

Gentleness: *Who is wise and understanding among you? Let him show by good conduct that his works are done in the meekness of wisdom.* James 3:13

Self-Control: *No temptation has overtaken you except such as is common to man; but God is faithful, who will not allow you to be tempted beyond what you are able, but with the temptation will also make the way of escape, that you may be able to bear it.* 1 Corinthians 10:13

Stand fast therefore in the liberty by which Christ has made us free, and do not be entangled again with a yoke of bondage. Galatians 5:1

A friend told me about his pushy, manipulative, possessive, and jealous girlfriend. He told me that even though he saw these red flags and more, he was still going to remain in the relationship and was even considering marrying her. He knew what he wanted in a woman, and he knew this woman wasn't able to give him what he wanted. What's worse, he was pretty sure that nothing would change after they got married. I asked him if he'd prayed about his future with this woman. His reply was yes, but that God had not yet spoken to him about their future. He also said that he was praying for God to show him what to do. I asked him, "What makes you think that God hasn't already done that?"

I asked him again, "What more does God have to show you?" After a few moments of silence, he admitted that soon after he began praying for direction concerning this relationship, he started to notice these things about her. He just never put them together as signs from God or answers to his prayers.

> **RECOVERY TIP:**
> *You will find yourself dealing with the same kind of people you dealt with in the past. Be careful not to allow what is comfortable or comforting to lull you back into bondage.*

Having been there before, I had much sympathy for him. He was obviously frustrated because he wanted her to be Ms. Right, but she wasn't. What had the biggest impact on me was that he somehow felt guilty about being attracted to someone who he knew wasn't healthy or emotionally stable enough to be in a relationship. He thought it was his fault for attracting her or being attracted to her. He'd been in a disastrous relationship just a few years before with someone just like her.

He was in a position that many of us find ourselves in after we've healed from the wounds of broken relationships, romantic or platonic: attracted to and attracting the same types of people who hurt you in the past.

Matthew 12:43–45 says: "When an unclean spirit goes out of a man, he goes through dry places seeking rest, and finds none. Then he says, 'I will return to my house from which I came.' When he comes, he finds it empty, swept and put in order. Then he goes and takes with him seven other spirits more wicked than himself, and they enter and dwell there; and the last state of the man is worse than the first." This passage usually is applied to deliverance from spiritual demonic possession but can also be applied to deliverance from emotional "demons" as well. Those demonic spirits come to do nothing but torment. Similarly, "familiar" spirits from past relationships also come to torment.

After you've healed emotionally and are spiritually stronger, you may find yourself dealing with the same types of people from your past. You have to be careful that you don't allow what is comfortable and comforting to lull you back into emotional and spiritual bondage. We who are stronger should pray for God to fill those "empty" spaces with his love, peace, grace, and mercy. Only then can we effectively witness to those who are hurting and seeking a safe sanctuary for truth with the hope that they will eventually be healed.

Post-Love Hangover Reflection

IN THE TIME I'VE SPENT restoring my relationship with God, I've finally realized one solution to my attracting and being attracted to the same type of men. It was because I hadn't allowed God to fill my empty spaces. I'd made some changes but not been obedient and spent the intimate time necessary with God to have a great spiritual harvest. Once I understood and made changes in my prayer and consecration time and began to submit myself more to the guidance and direction of the Holy Spirit, my emptiness was filled, and my life changed.

Chapter 13

Toxic People and
How to Avoid Them

---

*If I run into another man with "issues" that they haven't
dealt with, I'm going to scream. I'm so disappointed because
I know there are good men out there. I don't believe like
some people that men like my dad are nonexistent in the
younger generation. Most people have some "issues" from
the past, but most men that I've met are so quick to try to
disguise what are some real serious relationship problems
with "game." I told one guy if he wanted to play games, they
had plenty for sale at Toys R Us.*

AFTER MY LOVE HANGOVER, I took a break from dating.
During my sabbatical, I decided that I wanted to know how
to spot toxic people who create toxic relationships. My search took
me to 2 Timothy 3:2–7, which clearly lists types of people with
whom you should avoid being in a close and intimate relationship.
It's not that they aren't good to you, but because of their own
"stuff" and emotional baggage, it would be unhealthy and
dangerous for you to become emotionally entangled with them.

"For men will be lovers of themselves, lovers of money, boasters, proud, blasphemers, disobedient to parents, unthankful, unholy, unloving, unforgiving, slanderers, without self-control, brutal, despisers of good, traitors, headstrong, haughty, lovers of pleasure rather than lovers of God—having a form of godliness but denying his power."

2 Timothy 3:2–4

> **RECOVERY TIP:**
> *Take a break from dating. Everyone carries their own emotional baggage—it would be unhealthy and dangerous for you to become entangled again right away.*

What a list! There are at least sixteen different character flaws pointed out. Keep in mind that character differs from personality. Your character is the foundation for your personality and your personality traits. These sixteen traits refer to character flaws, not personality traits. There are obviously more, but these are some of the most serious. How can you tell the difference? Character flaws will eventually force you to look long and hard at yourself and how you affect other people. *Character flaws are much harder to fix and change.* Personality traits are rooted in character flaws and often act as a cover for those flaws.

For example, a personality flaw that I've worked hard to fix is that I'm *critical and (sometimes) judgmental*. A personality trait that springs from this foundation is that I'm overly analytical. As an English major, this turned out to be an asset when analyzing literature. However, in a relationship, it causes problems with communication and jumping to conclusions.

Be honest and stop being naive. God will show you the good and bad about your relationship and yourself. It's up to you to do something constructive with the truth.

Here are eight types of toxic people with biblical examples who can destroy you and your relationships:

The Bellywarmer

With her enticing speech she caused him to yield,
With her flattering lips she seduced him. . . . she has cast down
many wounded, And all who were slain by her were strong men.

Proverbs 7:21, 26

The bellywarmer knows that she is in the relationship for short-lived but highly gratifying pleasures. Perhaps because they were victimized by others in the past, bellywarmers are persons who are so good at victimizing others that they undermine any hope of stability and connection in a relationship.

Delilah, Samson's girlfriend in the Old Testament, is perhaps the best biblical example of a bellywarmer. Knowing that he was in love with her, others noticed the influence she had on him and asked her to help deliver him into the hands of the Philistines. Out of greed and perhaps her desire to please others, Delilah willingly agreed and set about to find out the source of Samson's strength.

In relationships, the bellywarmer spends the bulk of her energy proving how she is "so into" you and the relationship. Her unhealthy and unrelenting passion is more about the ultimate goal of gaining dominance over you. Sadly, she attempts to gain dominance over you when you are the weakest and most vulnerable. Much like Delilah, who asked Samson, "How can you lie to me when you say you love me?" your bellywarmer will also remain focused on your feelings conveniently omitting her feelings for you. Her goal, cleverly clouded by her exceptional ability to feed your carnal mind and flesh, is to control. Selfishness is one of her main motivators to either create, sustain, or end relationships.

Five Signs of a Bellywarmer

1. Has mastered the art of manipulating the emotions of others to get what he/she wants.
2. Offers to tell you "secrets" about others but insists she will keep "secrets" about you.
3. Seems oblivious to the presence of deceit and other sins in the relationship. Will often compromise using the reasoning "the ends justify the means."
4. Attracts and is often attracted to leader types who are independent thinkers and strong-willed; generally a follower. Intrigued and challenged, ironically, by the prospect of "conquering" or controlling another person.
5. Complains about the shortcomings of others without acknowledging that she may have the same flaws; hypocritical.

> **RECOVERY TIP:**
> *Recognize that no one is perfect. But don't ignore the red flags you notice about yourself and others.*

Faithful are *the wounds of a friend.*
But the kisses of an enemy are *deceitful.* Proverbs 27:6

Much like her biblical counterpart, the bellywarmer works extremely hard at overcoming difficult circumstances to remain in a position of perceived or anticipated control of others. She is glad to warm your "belly" with money, sex, attention, and compliments—all temporary pleasures. However, real relationship develops when the focus becomes the permanent, not the temporary. Because she has so often been controlled by others, she does the same in an intimate relationship with another.

The Great Pretender 4

> They profess to know God, but in works
> they deny Him, being abominable, disobedient, and disqualified
> for every good work. Titus 1:16

"It wasn't me." These words from a song by reggae artist Shaggy are also some of the most favorite phrases used by the great pretender, who through manipulation, denial, and keeping secrets, twists/denies the truth and causes a love hangover.

In fact, this person knows the truth and will fool you into believing that he both acknowledges and advocates the truth. However, what you'll find is that he will use you and his fragmented versions of "the truth" to satisfy his own desires. He often talks about and pretends to embrace the truth; however, whenever it is convenient, he will twist and even deny the truth. The great pretender will use a counterfeit truth to hide the truth about himself.

Peter, the disciple who denied Jesus three times, is a good example of the character of the great pretender. It was out of his fear of the consequences of truthfully acknowledging Jesus that Peter denied him. What was even more destructive was Peter's highly perfectionistic standards that caused him to experience tremendous amounts of stress. Matthew 26:34–35 describes him emphatically arguing that he would never deny Jesus. But verses 69 through 74 of the same chapter show a hostile and defensive Peter transformed to brokenheartedness, who weeps bitterly at the truth of Jesus' statements coming to pass and of his disobedience in denying the truth.

For the great pretender, having unrealistic standards for behavior will lead him to sometimes go into denial because the pain of the truth is too unbearable. He practices the unhealthy habit of twisting the truth, which always causes emotional devastation.

Five Signs of the Great Pretender

1. Places unrealistically high expectations on himself and others. Idealizes and romanticizes unsafe situations and unhealthy relationships. Highly perfectionistic and often inflexible.

> **RECOVERY TIP:**
> *Be honest with yourself. The growth and freedom you experience will be in direct relationship to how much you acknowledge the truth and how much you try to change.*

2. Experiences extreme emotional and mood swings. Usually sees situations and people in terms of being an asset or liability.

3. Struggles with the fear of rejection and is afraid of being out of control.

4. Will erase and delete uncomfortable and unmanageable situations, people, and memories. Has a difficult time properly grieving parts of the past.

5. Successfully convinces others to join him as he lives in denial. More comfortable living in the bondage of denial than enjoying the freedom of truth.

> *. . . having a form of godliness but denying its power.*
> *And from such people turn away.* 2 Timothy 3:5

Ironically, the perfectionistic great pretender will settle for much less than perfect in romantic relationships. His fear of failure motivates him to choose partners that he knows will never achieve his unrealistic standards. In turn, he is able to easily shift the focus from himself and to his relationship partner and her shortcomings.

For the best chance of success, relationships have to be based on truth and honesty. One of the great pretender's character flaws is he is so focused on being "perfect" rather than the more realistic goal of being "honest." What often happens is that the great pretender's relationships end up being frustrating and centered on chasing the unattainable.

The Cowardly Liar 4

A wholesome tongue is a tree of life,
But perverseness in it breaks the spirit. Proverbs 15:4

Just like a strong and healthy athlete can be injured during physical exercise through no fault of their own, so can a strong and healthy person be injured in relationships. Because of her crafty and deceptive nature, the cowardly liar has the potential to hurt people who are otherwise healthy and strong.

Manipulative and controlling are two adjectives that appropriately describe this person. Fueling her need for control is her fear. It could be a fear of intimacy and it could also be a fear of the pain that truth causes. Because the influence of fear in a relationship is so far-reaching, it can affect both the good and bad parts of the relationship, without even the healthy person realizing it. Sadly, because this fear has been ingrained over time or through emotionally devastating circumstances, the cowardly liar lets fear control nearly every aspect of her life. The cowardly liar uses lies to cover her fear. And, out of the envy of others that she is in relationship with who are not held in bondage to fear, she attempts to control their lives.

Often this person is very charismatic and very much a "people person"—ironically using the energy from other healthier people to sustain her in her cowardice. Her natural charisma often allows her to convince and manipulate others into taking credit or blame. Unable to deal with the burden of emotional responsibility, she persuades others to act as emotional shields for her. By persuasion and even coercion, she convinces others that it is in their best interests to help her. She usually can read you and others so well that she intuitively knows how, when, and which buttons to push to move you to do the things she wants.

Five Signs of the Cowardly Liar

> **RECOVERY TIP:**
> *Do not assume that others are as honest as you are—people who are deceptive can easily cause a healthy person to stumble.*

1. Always has an answer and an excuse. Over time will change answers to the same question. Quick-thinking and intelligent.

2. Speaks in terms of the future ("When we get engaged," "When I get a job," etc.), knowing that it will keep you distracted from the fact that he/she is not being honest with you now.

3. Tends to give indirect and unclear answers. Gets defensive and often frustrated when pressed for clear, direct answers.

4. Talks in-depth about surface relationship issues. Unwilling and unable to connect emotionally.

5. Creates and maintains triangulated relationships in which friends and/or family heavily influence your relationship. Maintains unclear and fragmented emotional and spiritual boundaries with others.

> *Be strong and of good courage;*
> *do not be afraid, nor be dismayed, for the LORD your God*
> *is with you wherever you go.* Joshua 1:9

Because this person is motivated by fear, he/she is unable to connect with God and subsequently with others. It is foolish and wishful thinking on your part if you believe that this person can't connect with God but can connect with you. One of the reasons this person can cause a healthy person to stumble is because

"Good people are guided by their honesty; treacherous people are destroyed by their dishonesty"—Proverbs 11:3, *New Living Bible.* You may mistakenly assume that others are as honest with you as you are with them. The cowardly liar assumes the emotionally dangerous and unavailable position that others are as equally deceptive as he is.

Unlike the cowardly lion from *The Wizard of Oz,* the cowardly liar is not taking you on the "yellow brick road" to Oz. If you are not careful, the cowardly liar will take you on a sad path that may include emotional, physical, spiritual, and emotional devastation.

The Blame Shifter

"Every good gift and every perfect gift is from above,
and comes down from the Father of lights with whom there is
no variation or shadow of turning." James 1:16–17

To many, the scariest characteristic about vampire movies is that Dracula lives in the night looking for some vulnerable person from which he can suck the life and blood. For me, the most terrifying aspect of this fictional creation is his ability to change physical forms. By shifting shapes, Dracula can appear an ally when he is really an enemy. Because he is only interested in meeting his needs, he uses this ability to catch people off guard and place them in a vulnerable (and sometimes deadly) position.

Out of similar self-centeredness, the blame shifter also craftily shifts blame and responsibility for problems to others. Her constant changing and manipulation of facts makes her one of the most frustrating people with whom you can be in a relationship. Proud and arrogant at times, this person is usually so much in love with herself and her ability to always do what is "right" for herself and others, she has a hard time accepting failure.

There are many examples of blame shifting in the Bible, a popular one is Adam. He gives a clear but sad glimpse into the mind of the blame shifter when he shifts blame to God and Eve and makes the statement "The woman whom You gave to be with me, she gave me of the tree . . ." (Genesis 3:12). Like so many blame shifters, Adam was burdened by guilt and shame. He relied on his pride and understanding in an attempt to resolve the situation. What he did was further complicate the situation and further distance himself from God.

The blame shifter is also very judgmental of others and quite merciless and only shows grace and compassion when it will benefit her. She harshly criticizes others, using phrases like, "They should have known better" or "If it were me, I would have . . ." She has an extraordinary ability to distinguish and discern what is right and wrong in the lives of others. However, blame shifters have a hard time accepting any type of wrongs in their own life.

Five Signs of a Blame Shifter

1. Becomes disinterested unless the activities are focused on her. Will often make you feel guilty when the activities are not focused on her. Self-centered and me-oriented.
2. Is very encouraging and masterful in using words to get an emotional response from people, usually pity and guilt.
3. Often comes from a family where one or both parents is a blame shifter. As a child, the blame shifter can sense the disconnection between the parents and, as a result, feels an overwhelming amount of guilt for somehow causing this pain in their relationship.
4. Suffers from very low-esteem and has little self-respect, even though she may appear self-confident and successful in her jobs and/or school.

5. Often has a difficult time making choices—unsure about her ability to make good choices (jobs, relationships, etc.).

Her self-centered nature keeps the blame shifter emotionally disconnected. Those who choose to develop and pursue relationships with this person are often left feeling empty and wondering what they are doing wrong because of the lack of emotional connection.

> **RECOVERY TIP:**
> *Accept responsibility for your mistakes, and look for others to respect themselves and be responsible for their own attitudes.*

The blame shifter is often passionate in the initial stages of the relationship. She may call frequently and shower you with lots of attention. She works very hard to convince you to fall in love with her. However, the passion is influenced by her knowing that you will eventually love her as much as she loves herself. She is so much in love with herself that she thinks it's great that you agree with what a wonderful person she is. The "flutter" that you feel when you are with this person is a pleasant distraction from the fact that the blame shifter rarely accepts responsibility for her own mistakes, failures, and shortcomings. Just as she blames others for her problems, eventually she will also blame you.

The Running Man/Woman

> *But Jonah arose to flee to Tarshish*
> *from the presence of the LORD.* Jonah 1:3

We all know what this person looks like and often feel sorry him. He has so much potential that is seemingly wasted on his attempts to circumvent responsibility. Of course, this toxic person is the "running man or woman," someone who can cause emotional distress because of his instability and immaturity. This person is often fearful not of truth, but of the consequences of truth. This person is usually very intelligent, but ultimately uses his intelligence to thwart God's plan for his life. He often ends up doing the same to your life.

This person is usually attracted to people who are very giving and compassionate. Because he is self-absorbed and overly confident in his abilities, he is an expert at playing the victim and getting others to feel sorry for him.

What exactly is this person running from? One possible reason that he runs is because he knows the extent, burden, and benefit of God's calling on his life.

Five Signs of the Running Man/Woman

1. Shows no respect for rules and authority figures. Is attracted to the allure of twisting or changing rules. Irresponsible and prone to quitting jobs, leaving school and ending relationships unexpectedly.

2. Reacts to situations and avoids being assertive or taking the initiative to change. Judgmental of others who are more emotionally mature and aggressive. Has very little faith that some situations and circumstances will change.

3. Will unwittingly and sometimes on purpose bring storms into the lives of others to whom he is closest. Sees this as an unfortunate consequence of relationship. Ironically, others will turn to God after seeing the storms in the running man/woman's life. The running man realizes, though doesn't always admit it, that he is the cause.

4. Remains aloof and emotionally detached which makes ending relationships, leaving jobs, and moving from uncomfortable circumstances easier. Often relies on his

inner dialogue to make decisions, unusually reliant on his own opinions of situations. Oblivious to the pain of others.

5. Appears very satisfied with his current status. Not interested in change because it appears too difficult. Very good at creating excuses for not growing.

Remember, the running man/woman's running is not confusion or lack of focus. It is merely disobedience, which has severe and lifechanging consequences for those who choose to follow its path or be with those who follow its path.

The Blended Smoothie

The words of his mouth were smoother than butter,
But war was in his heart; His words were softer than oil,
Yet they were drawn swords. Psalm 55:21

An enduring cultural phenomenon from the 1990s was the smoothie drink, a fruit or vegetable-flavored drink with various fruits and vegetables all blended together to create a new taste, one that often promised better taste than the original ingredients by themselves. Likewise, the blended smoothie is a person who takes bits and pieces from past relationships into their new relationships in an effort to build up their dreadfully low self-esteem.

Because she can dialogue on a variety of topics and cultural issues, the blended smoothie deceives others into believing they have great personal, spiritual, financial, and emotional depth. In fact, she is very shallow and needy. Sadly, she will take from others to maintain her life . . . without regard to how it will affect others. Like the drink often does, this person will eventually leave an unsettling aftertaste.

Five Signs of the Blended Smoothie

1. Has poor self-image that is masked by her diverse tastes. Often follows the advice of others. Believes that taking on the traits of others will fill the void that she feels.
2. Desperately seeks acceptance from others.
3. Can see the beauty in others, but not themselves.
4. Appears to like most, if not all, the things you like. Probably the most compatible person you've ever dated.
5. Sees intimacy as an improbable emotional reward in a relationship and is deceptively open.

Like King Solomon, this person is prone to being distracted easily by the behavior of others. She is open to alternative lifestyles, religious practices, and attitudes. While it is good to be open to new things, the blended smoothie will leave an aftertaste of idol worship and idle relationships. Most of her relationships are characterized as eccentric and temporarily exciting, but in the long term offer an aftertaste of emptiness.

The Locksmith

> *While they promise them liberty, they themselves*
> *are slaves of corruption; for by whom a person is overcome,*
> *by him also he is brought into bondage.* 2 Peter 2:19

How often do you need a locksmith? Not too often—only in emergencies when you've gotten locked out of or locked into a situation that you can't get yourself out of. Even though you are relieved when they do their job, what you feel in the in-between time is an overwhelming sense of helplessness and powerlessness. The power that we feel is usually when we admire the power that the locksmith has.

Control is the overwhelming concern of the locksmith. Because either his family background or relationship experiences resulted in a loss of trust, the locksmith has a difficult time trusting. This loss of trust is more exaggerated in his close and intimate relationships, usually because this reminds him of an experience in the past when someone trusted took advantage of or betrayed his trust.

Five Signs of a Locksmith

1. Tends to be extremely controlling—spiritually, physically, emotionally and financially. Very demanding early on in the relationship that you trust him completely.
2. Usually attracts and is attracted to people who have a weakened vision (or no vision at all) for their life. Good at explaining a well-detailed and convincing vision for his life, your life, and your relationship.
3. Eager to convince you that he will make the difficult areas of your life easier to cope with. Often shows this by taking charge of things with and without your permission.
4. Sometimes has a difficult time accepting direction from authority figures, all the while demanding that you submit to his leadership.
5. Appeals to our basic human need for security and safety.

Ironically, the locksmith is focused on earning and then controlling your trust, not because he treasures trust, but because he treasures the power that comes from being trusted. This person finds comfort in being your lifeline and having the keys to your everything. He feels an overwhelming emptiness when he doesn't feel needed.

The Snail

The woman said to Him, "Sir, give me this water,
that I may not thirst, nor come here to draw." John 4:15

The snail is like the driver of the car: she knows where she's going, how soon she wants to get there, and when the trip ends. Most significantly, the snail is in control of the passenger's destination. The snail appears to be on the path of commitment. However, she is taking her time and is in no rush to seriously commit. This person will live with you for years without marrying you or keep you guessing when she will say the magical words, "I love you."

The Samaritan woman at the well is a good example of this toxic personality. The fact that she has had six past relationships with the most recent not being her husband, indicates that she craved the security of commitment, but was ultimately frightened by committing to the wrong person. The snail is highly perfectionistic and keeps a mental Rolodex of your unqualifications. She is in no rush to tell you why you are not qualified. She will just give you "time" to change without honestly sharing with you what will happen if you don't.

Five Signs of the Snail

1. Enjoys the power and attention of your becoming more and more attached to her. Doesn't discourage your deepening commitment. Self-centered.
2. Has a history of enjoying spiritual, physical, financial, and emotional benefits of relationship without the responsibility.
3. Tends to notice and point out differences quickly. Suspicious and uncomfortable with those differences.

4. Settles or compromises in various areas of her life with the rationalization that something better will come along. Quick to seek things that she assumes are better.

5. Recognizes truth in many situations; however her history of compromise keeps her from following the truth.

The snail likes being in a position of controlling the emotional flow of the relationship by having something tangible or intangible that the other person wants. She often will allow normal distractions to destroy relationships and the lives of those who care about her.

Post-Love Hangover Reflection

THROUGH MY OWN RELATIONSHIP EXPERIENCES, I see that people play games in relationships to gain or maintain an unfair advantage over their "love." Why would someone play games with you and your heart? Sometimes the answer is as simple as this: you let them and you don't protect yourself. Sometimes the answer is more complicated because it involves trying to understand the motivations of others—they may feel powerless and try to gain their perceived loss of power by manipulating you. Based on how they were raised, they may not know any other way of dealing with relationships.

If you are the victim of relationship games, the reasons don't really matter: getting revenge does. Games, by their nature, often involve a declared winner and loser. The sad thing about relationship games is that you may declare yourself the "winner" by taking advantage of someone else's vulnerable heart. But what have you really won?

Whispers of Love

Pause for Reflection

Signs that You May Be Over Your Love Hangover

1. You are no longer angry when you think about your ex.
2. You are no longer angry or feel hurt when you think about the relationship.
3. You no longer call your ex or accept his/her phone calls, and you no longer have dreams, visions, fantasies about retaliation and revenge.
4. You are no longer distracted in your mind or inquire about how your ex is doing.
5. You are able to talk about your ex without crying or getting emotionally upset.
6. You no longer yearn for the relationship to be reconciled and for things to be the way they were.
7. You can now look at pictures, cards, and souvenirs from the relationship without feeling angry, guilty, or ashamed, etc.
8. You are able to enjoy your normal routine.
9. You no longer call your ex's home, job, or friends and hang up.
10. You no longer drive by your ex's job or home hoping to catch a glimpse of him/her.

11. You no longer demand or expect an apology from your ex.
12. You embrace safe and healthy relationships with the opposite sex.
13. You no longer avoid public places from fear that you'll see him/her.
14. Memories of the relationship bring a smile, not a sting.
15. You no longer fear and avoid intimacy.
16. You can accept both the good and bad things about the relationship and your ex.
17. You have regained your appetite and lost and/or gained weight.
18. Your sleeping patterns have returned to normal.
19. You no longer blame your ex for current, past, or future relationship problems.
20. You drop all strategies to actively break up his/her new relationship.

Out of the list above, choose the three that were easiest and the three that were the hardest for you to reach.

Is anything too hard for the LORD?
Genesis 18:14

Name at least three reasons why you think these were easy or hard to achieve.

Hatred stirs up strife, But love covers all sins.

Proverbs 10:12

In what ways could you show God's love and compassion to your ex if the situation arose?

For You are my hope, O Lord GOD;
You are my trust from my youth.

Psalm 71:5

How did you feel God's grace during and after your breakup?

Oh, give thanks to the LORD, for He is good!
For His mercy endures forever.

1 Chronicles 16:34

Describe three good and three bad things about the relationship for which you are grateful.

What brings you the most hope as you think about your future relationships?

Part 6

AFFIRMATION

*It is good to give thanks
to the LORD,
And to sing praises to Your name,
O Most High;
To declare Your lovingkindness
in the morning,
And Your faithfulness every night.*

Psalm 92:2

"No justice, no peace."
—*Al Sharpton*

In the quest for a peaceful love hangover recovery, there is a temptation to minimize wrongs and to justify poor behavior. Our spirits seek, desire, and need peace. Not feeling at peace is disruptive. You might have trouble sleeping, communicating, and making decisions. Acknowledging a wrong is the first step to achieving peace. The many grudges you have held inside can create a tear in your own integrity. Writing them down helps clear up what the issues really are. In some instances, you may have justifiable anger, resentment, or even cause for legal action. In others, you may have magnified something insignificant that was masking the real issue. Be honest. Allow ample time. It is okay to come back to the list and make changes. As you deal with your own conscience, the truth may be revealed in areas where you have lied even to yourself.

As your thoughts become clear on who you are not at peace with, say out loud:

> I release _____. What _____ did was not right and may never be corrected. I may never receive an apology. This issue no longer has the power to take away my peace. As I release _____, I feel myself healing more and more from what he/she did. I am giving this issue the appropriate attention it deserves. I invite peace into my life. I value peace. I seek peace and welcome peace between me and _____."

If it is possible, as much as depends on you, live peaceably with all men. Romans 12:18

Chapter 14

How Does Your Garden Grow?

I can't believe it! It's been a year since my ex and I broke up. Not that I didn't think a year would come, but because I'm surprised at how much growth I've made in a short amount of time. I see that there was a purpose in the pain that I experienced. I never would have believed that God could have turned my pain into something good for me. I know the Scripture about God turning all things to good, but I didn't want to believe it. I now see that there is a purpose in my pain. I spent the last year working to make myself better.

T HE MORE TIME I SPENT IN PRAYER, the more I felt like I should share my story with others. Occasionally, I reread my journals for encouragement that I was making progress. Once when I read them, I said aloud, "That would make an interesting book." I laughed the first time I said it. The second time, the realization that the Lord wanted me to share my recovery experience with others coursed through my spirit and soul. Of course, I wasn't yet willing or ready to do so, but God just wouldn't let me forget about it.

I was having lunch with the publisher of *The Dallas Weekly* when he casually asked the question, "When are you going to start writing for me?" It took me a few seconds to recover. He didn't know that the Lord had placed in my heart writing about my relationship recovery experience for his paper less than a month earlier. I kept hesitating because I didn't think I was ready to deal with the aftermath of writing about that very private area of my life. I tried to convince myself that I was losing my mind to even think about baring my most intimate details with anyone other than my close friends and family. He merely confirmed that I would be crazy to do any different.

As I was preparing for this task, one song kept coming to mind, "Love Hangover," by Diana Ross. As a child I wondered why someone wouldn't want a cure for something that hurt them. I also thought of a favorite childhood nursery rhyme that brought great insight to my writing. The rhyme questions, "How does your garden grow?" When asked about my emotions, this question forced me to take a good, honest look at what I had done to restore my brokenness and love-hungry emotional garden to true emotional health.

A healthy emotional garden is cultivated ground that is used as the foundation and soil for a healthier future. Having a healthy garden will help as you prepare for maturity and spiritual growth. In the Bible, gardens were places of intimacy and contemplation. This is where the communion with God took place with Adam (Genesis 2:8) and also at the Garden of Gethsemane with Jesus (Matthew 26:36).

A number of things are needed for your garden:

- Tools
- Activity
- The right position or perspective

A hoe and gloves are instruments needed to prepare an area for gardening. The hoe acts as a blunt instrument to break up the dry and resistant soil. Similarly, the word of God, which we receive either by reading or hearing from others, breaks up the hard, fallow ground. The gloves are for safety and protection from unseen elements in the soil. I wear gloves when I clean to protect my hands from the harsh chemicals, and I'm always amazed by how much dirt is left on the gloves when I'm finished. The word of God acts as a "glove" for our emotions and protects us from unseen dangers through the wisdom of the word.

The activities that take place in a garden, like hoeing and planting, are surprisingly isolated by nature. You usually work a garden by yourself. When Jesus went to the Garden of Gethsemane, the disciples were nearby, but when he was praying most intently, he was by himself. Don't avoid your seasons of isolation.

A gardener must be constant and tenacious. Even after planting the seeds, a good gardener will check for weeds and make sure that the seeds are still germinating. When seeking emotional healing, we must use this same type of persistence in our prayer time. Praying without ceasing must become a goal. By praying constantly, we take our minds off of the immediacy of the problem and place them on the hope of the solution which is in Christ Jesus.

The right depth mirrors our level of intimacy with God. How deep you till the soil determines the effectiveness of the preparation. You can pull up weeds at the roots and get rid of the rocks. The deeper you dig, the better the chances the foundation will be solid. Likewise, how deeply you pray determines the foundation for your spiritual walk. Will it be full of weeds because you only touched the surface and did not dig into the roots? The foundation will also determine how deeply rooted the seeds you plant will become.

> RECOVERY TIP:
> **Two things will help you grow: the tears of your disappointment, which are a sign of release and a natural part of recovery, and the light of God's truth, which dispels the darkness.**

"Those who sow in tears will reap with songs of joy. He who goes out weeping carrying seed to sow, will return with songs of joy, carrying sheaves with him." Psalms 126:5–6 NIV

Two things that help a garden grow are water and sunshine. Water provides the moisture and nourishment. Our tears during times of great disappointment and sadness often result from us allowing our hearts to be touched by God. The tears result, oftentimes, from the internal struggle that takes place as we struggle against the truths he is showing us about ourselves. The tears are signs of emotional release and a natural part of the recovery process. As the tears flow, we experience a slow shift as the emotional expression brings us closer to God.

"The LORD will guide you always; he will satisfy your needs in a sun-scorched land and will strengthen your frame. You will be like a well-watered garden, like a spring whose waters never fail." Isaiah 58:11 NIV

Sunshine is the light that is provided by God's truth. Truth is found in God's word, and the freedom of truth comes also from the words of encouragement from others. The light into the garden will dispel our emotional darkness, not the other way around.

Fifteen Important Things I Learned about Myself
While Growing My Garden:

1. I was emotionally strengthened by going through my love hangover.
2. I have good judgment.
3. I have self-respect.
4. I am a God-fearing and God-loving woman.
5. I am a valuable friend.
6. I am a valuable relationship partner.
7. I value friendships.
8. I need emotional support.
9. I can experience joy after living in the valley of pain.
10. Trust and truth are important to me.
11. Love is an emotion that involves choice based on truth.
12. Boundaries are important, for myself and for others.
13. I can have boundaries and stick to them as the relationship progresses.
14. Once married, sexuality will be a part of me that I can embrace rather than fear.
15. I am a recovering codependent.

"So now what? You've been told the many signs and symptoms of a love hangover, shared personal experiences along with rather realistic fictional scenarios, and even traversed through the shortcomings and skeletons seemingly in my past, stepping on a couple of my toes! Like many others who are suffering a love hangover, I'm asked the question "How do I even begin to cope?" My response is the self search method. The key is to be *pro*active in the recovery, not reactive. This gave me a newfound sense of control in my emotional well-being. I was able to appreciate a sense of control I felt that I lost at some point towards the end of my relationship.

The Self-Search Method

Search self.

Externalize those emotions!

Love self.

Console your soul.

Forgive him/her.

Denounce animosity.

Seek understanding.

Be encouraged.

Regain self-confidence.

Know that the heart is not so smart.

Do not seek love or attempt to manufacture it haphazardly.
The pain remains.

Do not use a new companion as a temporary Band-Aid or
crutch. The pain remains.

Realize that the pain remains. The remedy? Time and
acceptance

Use this disappointment as a stepping stone.

Use that river of tears for swimming out of misery into a safe
harbor.

Remember the pleasurable past, recognize the painful
present, but realize that tomorrow promises a new day.

Embrace wisdom gained from such an unpleasant experience.

Respect the potential vulnerability an emotional attachment
often brings.

Have the courage to wake up alone.

Understand being alone and loneliness are *not* the same.

Understand that the script had already been written; you
were merely a playing your role.

Be an optimist, yet a realist.

Deal with those demons.

Do not feel victimized, but sanitized.

Do not ask what, why, or how, but be thankful you survived!

Respect and desire unconditional love.

Stay encouraged.

Seek inner peace.

Calm the storm.

Recite the Serenity Prayer.

Emancipate your heart, body, mind and
 soul.

Love self

Love yourself.

You must love *yourself!*

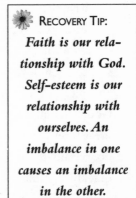

Recovery Tip:
Faith is our relationship with God. Self-esteem is our relationship with ourselves. An imbalance in one causes an imbalance in the other.

Three essential spiritual elements to a successful love hangover remedy and for effective implementation of the self-search method are: faith, trust and esteem.

Faith deals with our relationship with God—it is upward. Trust centers around our relationship with others and is horizontal. Self-esteem is our relationship with ourselves and is inward. Because these three are interconnected, an imbalance with any one can negatively affect the others. Working in balance, these three provide the keys for restoration and rebuilding.

> *Then Jesus said to him, "Go your way; your faith*
> *has made you well." And immediately he received his sight*
> *and followed Jesus on the road.* Mark 10:52

Faith is probably the most crucial of the three because it helps establish a relationship with God. As much as I hated (and sometimes still do) to admit, I allowed the loss of the relationship with my ex-boyfriend to affect my faith in God. It was difficult to continue to have "faith" in God when he didn't do the things that I prayed he should. Not only was I disappointed in myself for my part in the relationship ending, I was also disappointed that (1) God would allow me to be hurt again and (2) to not have shown me that the relationship would end.

Faith was very hard for me as I attempted to deal with my disappointment. I even turned away from God during the early stages of my love hangover. I used my emotional disappointment and pity as rationale and justification for distancing myself from God. After all, I had believed God when he said that he would do great things in our relationship. I had faith that God was going to do certain things, and he didn't. After the breakup, my attitude quickly became, "Why should I have faith in God, who didn't allow what he knew I wanted so desperately to happen?" I was angry at God. I continued to pray that he would deliver me from those negative emotions, but, ironically, I stopped attending church services.

> *Therefore, since we have been justified through faith,*
> *we have peace with God through our Lord Jesus Christ.*
> Romans 5:1, NIV

My anger, though unexpressed was so easy to spot. I had lost faith because of my anger. I realized that it is difficult to have faith when you are angry. I felt guilty and ashamed of my anger at God. I was angry because this situation had left me feeling powerless. Once I acknowledged and embraced these negative feelings, and I realized that I was angry not at God, but because I felt powerless, my faith in God was restored. And when my faith in God, his word, and his promises was restored, I was able and willing to begin the healing process.

"Behold, God is my salvation, I will trust, and not be afraid;
'for YAH, the LORD, is my strength and song; . . .' " Isaiah 12:2

Trust. It's amazing how a word so easy to spell and pronounce can have such a profound effect on us and our relationships. Trust will:

- Determine the level of intimacy in a relationship, romantic or platonic
- Provide the foundation for a relationship, romantic or platonic
- Change the boundaries in a relationship, romantic or platonic
- Change perceptions about ourselves, others, and our relationships

Trust, like a double-edged sword, cuts both ways and can be used as a weapon to both arm and disarm you and your relationship partner. Think about how many times you hear the phrase "I just don't trust him/her" spoken by others as they describe their relationship. By trusting someone with your dreams, moments of triumph and sadness, and the most intimate details of your life, you place yourself in a vulnerable position. If the person in whom you've placed trust is trustworthy, safe, and shares the same with you, then you will experience a fulfilling relationship that will positively impact your life. But if you place trust in someone who is not trustworthy, who is unsafe and does not share intimately, you place yourself in a dangerously vulnerable position that has the potential to destroy your life.

God allowed me to struggle, and then he blessed me to win the struggle with trusting others in my life. Many people assumed that because I wasn't dating anyone, I had decided that no one can be trusted. However, I pointed out to them that because I trusted my father and mother, I would always believe that I could have that same type of trusting relationship with others.

A mistake I made with my ex-boyfriend was giving my trust prematurely, rather than making him earn it. Because he was so charming and was willing to spend so much time in developing a relationship, I got distracted in the whirlwind of attention and love he showed me. As a result, when the relationship ended, I felt so empty and I had a very difficult time establishing relationships with others.

Trust in the LORD with all your heart. And lean not on
your own understanding; in all your ways acknowledge Him,
And He shall direct your paths. Proverbs 3:5–6

I knew that eventually I would be vulnerable and open with others. I was just uncertain with whom and when. But God placed new friends in my life and showed me how to develop safe and healthy relationships. These friends worked to show me that they were trustworthy and valued my trust.

Once I was able to wisely discern toxic people, I began to research what healthy men and women are like and what a healthy relationship is like. My research led me to the majestic biblical love story of Ruth and Boaz. Through divine connection and circumstance, Ruth and Boaz exemplified the legacy of the obedience to God's greater plan. They represent the epitome of the healthy, godly relationship between a man and a woman.

The Old Testament book of Ruth provides good examples of what men and women should look for in the opposite sex when seeking romantic or platonic relationships. Characters like Ruth and Boaz illustrate through their actions and words the positive traits that we should look for when we consider developing a trusting and intimate relationship with someone.

Ruth, her mother-in-law, and her sister-in-law are attempting to rebuild their lives after the devastating deaths of their respective spouses and sons. Ruth is determined to remain with Naomi, her mother-in-law, and be a part of her life. The rest of the story details her intriguing courtship and eventual marriage to Boaz.

Through this courtship we see Ruth grow from a grief-stricken widow into a confident woman, which is a perfect example of what women, single or married, should be. Though not perfect, she provides a good illustration of a woman who seeks growth in the spiritual, financial and emotional areas of her life.

Here are the healthy characteristics that Ruth demonstrates:

> **RECOVERY TIP:**
> *A healthy woman and a healthy man exhibit healthy personal traits and characteristics. Learn what they are and look for them in your relationships.*

Twelve Signs of a Healthy Woman

1. Rather than being held captive to her past or past mistakes, she recognizes the blessings found in the second chances that God gives.
2. She values relationships and strives to maintain relationships with others. She is open to developing new relationships with others.
3. She seeks the advice of others and applies this advice to her individual situation or circumstance. She values and seeks the counsel of wiser elders
4. She is willing to submit to spiritual, professional, and personal relationships.
5. She is willing and able to provide financially for herself. Also, she seeks to take care of those who are less fortunate.

6. She is not afraid of stepping our of her comfort zone and relying on faith, not fear, as she pursues future goals.

7. She is not too proud to show gratitude and thanks for the kindness of others.

8. She is obedient to the word of God.

9. She has healthy emotional and spiritual boundaries and respects the boundaries of others.

10. She seeks honesty in relationships.

11. She can handle being humbled by God and is willing to mature.

12. She is in touch with and willing to express her emotions. She is honest about the impact of emotions like joy, doubt, and fear.

One impact of Ruth's story is that we see her grow and can identify with her working through her insecurities as she grows.

Through actions and words, Boaz depicts an emotionally healthy, godly man. As a businessman and ultimately kinsman redeemer for Ruth, Boaz illustrates the positive impact that a healthy relationship partner can have in your life. Boaz does not jump to conclusions about Ruth, but decides to find out for himself. He patiently deals with her and does his best to be understanding of her situation.

Boaz knows many things about Ruth through what he's heard from others, but he also observes Ruth for himself and takes note of her behavior and her character. He recognizes her godliness and her desire to remain focused on God's will for her life. An unhealthy man would feel threatened and inadequate with a woman who possesses a strong spiritual life, but Boaz appreciates that Ruth loves the Lord.

Because an emotionally balanced man desires to walk upright and strong, he will realize that this trait can enhance his walk and spiritual journey. He will admire, not mock, a woman who desires to have a stronger relationship with God.

Twelve Signs of a Healthy Man

1. He is protective without being possessive.
2. He does not attempt to control or manipulate the thoughts, attitudes, or opinions of others; nor does he allow himself to be controlled or manipulated by the thoughts, attitudes, or opinions of others.
3. He is nonjudgmental about his past and your past as well.
4. He is obedient to God's will for his life and encourages others to do the same.
5. He respects boundaries—emotional, physical, spiritual, and financial.
6. He is honest, open, straightforward, and direct in personal and professional relationships.
7. He follows through on promises he makes.
8. He helps those who are vulnerable, emotionally and spiritually; he discourages others from taking advantage of those who are emotionally and spiritually vulnerable.
9. He is an ambitious visionary who strives to follow the God-given plan for his life, and he encourages other to do the same.
10. He is patient and not easily frustrated.
11. He is generous with his time, talents, and treasure, and he is not prone to selfishness or selfish actions.
12. He notices when others need love, honor, respect, and compassion. He willingly gives emotional support to others without expecting anything in return, and he can handle being an emotional anchor for others.

Rather than look for the romantic ideal of the knight in shining armor, women should look for someone who is striving to be a godly man and who seeks God's will. The biblical character of Boaz shows that a man who seeks after God will provide more than just financial rewards for himself and those with whom he is in relationship.

Ruth and Boaz show the blessings that occur when both partners strive for emotional and spiritual health. Their relationship depicts how healthy relationships accept a God-given vision of obedience. It also shows how a healthy relationship establishes clear and firm boundaries. A healthy relationship is inclusive and not isolated. Additional signs are a nonhurried pace, accountability, and a pursuit of purpose.

Ruth and Boaz know of their unique family connection and of his chance to be Ruth's kinsman redeemer. Neither rush their desire to be together. Ruth takes Naomi's advice and then patiently waits for Boaz. She could have spoken with the close relative, but she waits for Boaz to take the initiative. This pace is comfortable for both—one doesn't manipulate and demand that the other comply. Interestingly, we also see Ruth guiding the level of intimacy in the relationship. She chooses to open up to Boaz *after* she sees that he is caring, generous, and worthy of her trust. By giving the relationship time to develop its foundation, Ruth seeks an emotional anchor. Her patience ensures that both she and Boaz are filling their emotional voids with God and not people.

Rather than seeking approval from their community of family and friends, Ruth and Boaz choose instead to be accountable to their community. They both make public their interest in the other—Ruth when she speaks to Naomi and Boaz when he meets with the elders at the gate. By keeping their relationship public, they avoid the pitfall of developing a relationship characterized by secrets, the seeds of deception.

Both people in a relationship should have professional, personal, and spiritual goals. These goals often change as we mature through seasons of our life. Eventually, they will extend beyond possessing material things. Their initial purpose can include starting a family and financial stability, but it should not end with these goals. Ruth and Boaz see the opportunity to assist each other in achieving their God-given purpose. Their purposes are interdependent, not codependent, and encourage faith-filled steps of growth. Their purpose is "now-centered" and a part of the future-oriented vision by God for both of their lives.

A healthy relationship will show godly love, not carnal lust; it will highlight goodness, not guilt; exemplify faithfulness, not fantasy; and spread gentleness, not ridicule. And it will be characterized by self-control and not self-centeredness. Respecting choice is key to laying the foundation for a healthy relationship. The ability to love and be a part of someone's life grows from seeds of emotional health. A healthy relationship will grow between two individuals and will encourage the same growth for others.

Post-Love Hangover Reflection

IT WAS ONLY THROUGH ADMITTING MY POWERLESSNESS that God miraculously restored my faith in him. How? I had to rely on something that was greater than the pain that I was experiencing . . . and that was God. The many times I prayed and cried out to him to help me found me physically looking up (vertically) and asking, "Why?" The more I looked up during these times, physically and spiritually, the clearer it became that God was indeed with me. The more I prayed, the more I began to feel peace about the situation. I had to embrace the peace that God was so lovingly offering me. When I stopped looking down and began looking up to God, he restored my confidence in making wise relationship decisions and began to prepare me to enjoy future healthier relationships.

Chapter 15

A View from the Other Side

Yesterday, I read a passage of literature that reminds me so much of how I was fourteen months ago. It's from Sense and Sensibility. *Reading how Marianne cried so over her broken heart that she almost died reminds me of how I thought my life was over too. I'm more thankful than I ever thought I'd be that I didn't marry him. I'm more thankful now than I'd ever thought possible.*

S*ENSE AND* S*ENSIBILITY* IS ONE OF MY FAVORITE NOVELS, a great romantic novel by Jane Austen that describes the typical and not-so-typical ups and downs of provincial British life in the early 1800s. It cleverly describes the lives of Marianne and Elinor Dashwood as they navigate the rough waters of love.

This novel is fascinating and timeless because of its portrayal of the emotional and physical upheaval that Marianne, the younger sister, experiences when her love, Willoughby, abruptly ends their relationship and marries a wealthier woman. Marianne is emotionally unstable and subsequently experiences a deep depression that threatens her life, due in part to her bitterness, anger, and unexpressed emotional stress.

Austen shows the timeless truth in having emotional balance and the ferocious fight for spiritual and emotional health. Elinor's overly protective "big sister" reaction to a letter of "explanation" from Willoughby on his behavior was easier for me to appreciate after my season of healing:

> RECOVERY TIP:
> *Recognize the irony of having a love hangover—feeling cheated and deceived but still wanting to hang on to a relationship with a person who has made it clear that it's over.*

She dared not trust herself to speak, . . . lest she might wound Marianne still deeper by treating their disengagement . . . as an escape from the worst and most irremediable of all evils, a connection for life, with an unprincipled man, as a deliverance the most real, a blessing the most important.

The statement about pain and heartbreak being an escape from a more devastating life with a dishonorable man struck a chord with me. Rather than seeing the tears as a punishment and blaming myself, I needed to change my perspective. By seeking God's will, I was able to see that this man was not who I thought he was. In fact, God was showing me that this man would cause me harm. As you think about your "Willoughby," remember that it is better to shed tears over a broken heart for a season than to cry a river of tears for a lifetime.

The irony of a love hangover: "Hanging on" to that person despite the fact he made it undeniably clear it was over. Seems a bit uncanny and confusing. Obsessive. Even downright crazy! So why do so many people do it? Why is it so hard to wake up alone? The truth is, it varies from person to person. However, a common factor is that we feel cheated and deceived. Cheated of that happily-ever-after love story and deceived by misleading innuendoes, longed-for affection, romantic moments in time, pleasurable sex, and possibly conditional love. Feelings of being cheated and deceived serve as the firewood for the emotional inferno of anger that comes along with the mourning after.

The last thing we look for during the mourning of a love hangover is the mirror. Why is this? Maybe because the mirror doesn't lie. It only reflects reality. No innuendoes. No misinterpretations. No distortions. No lies. Crust and mascara matted to the corner of your eye, an ugly mole on the left side of your face, broccoli between your teeth. The mirror will reflect it all. Without bias. Facing that "mirror," the mourning after forces us to deal with our personal realities and holds us partly, if not totally, accountable. You might argue, "But it was all his fault! He lied to me!" or "She used me financially and left me dry!"

It may simply be that you learned a priceless lesson. You're still breathing. You're still standing. *Get on with living life!* Placing blame, investigating, playing detective, or desperately playing "let's make a deal" trying to get him or her back will only prolong your pain. Deal with the ugly reality of your heartache. It won't kill you. In fact, once you work through it, you will eventually find peace of mind. Release that emotional inferno! Cry, scream, punch, kick. Whatever you destroy in the house can be replaced a lot easier than your sanity. But I encourage you in your rage to use some control—Try to not break that mirror!

One thing I had to do was keep looking at myself—no matter how difficult—and courageously face what was staring back. The "view from the other side" is what you see when you courageously gaze into the mirror, stronger and healthier, with the determination to live as God intended—whole and holy!

One of my most treasured gifts is a figurine of a bride in a wedding dress holding a beautiful flower bouquet, given to me by my ex-boyfriend about three months before we broke up. I value this gift not for what it meant to me then, but for what it means to me now.

When I looked at this figurine a few Christmases ago, our breakup was still so painful that I packed it into a bag and threw it into the back of the closet. It stayed there until months later when I rediscovered it, dusted it off, and placed it on my entertainment center. Some of my friends thought that I should have mailed it to my ex and his new wife. I told them I hadn't done that because I knew one day I would see it as a nice figurine, not as a painful reminder of the past.

I wasn't sure how I'd work through my grief from broken promises, hurtful words, humiliating lies, and unfulfilled dreams. Had it not been for prayer, fasting, and reading the word of God, I don't know how I would have survived. That figurine no longer symbolizes what I lost. It now symbolizes what God lovingly gave me the strength to overcome.

God blessed me with the desire to be emotionally and spiritually healthy. Even more in his grace and his mercy, he granted my heart's desire to be whole again.

> *"Behold, I will do a new thing, Now it shall spring forth;*
> *Shall you not know it? I will even make a road*
> *in the wilderness And rivers in the desert."* Isaiah 43:19

Never put a question mark where God has put a period. This is a phrase that I've heard used when describing what our reaction should be to death. This phrase was even used by a funeral home in San Antonio as their promotional slogan. I have recently thought about how this phrase could also be applied to forgiveness (and unforgiveness).

The question mark indicates that there is more information that needs to be given, that there is a lack of understanding. In other words, the sentence implies something incomplete.

The period, on the other hand, signifies the end of the thought or thoughts in the sentence. It is complete. It also shows that another thought or idea is about to be introduced; something new is about to begin. Interestingly, you can replace a period with a question mark and change the entire meaning of a sentence. For example, "I have never seen the righteous forsaken?" has a very different meaning than "I have never seen the righteous forsaken."

Think of forgiveness and unforgiveness in much the same way:

> **RECOVERY TIP:**
> *Put the "period" of forgiveness on your lost relationship. Erase the "question mark" of unforgiveness so you can move on to a new relationship.*

- Forgiveness is a choice. One result of forgiveness is that there is no sting when you think about the situation, person, or experience. You may not completely let go of the memories, but you no longer allow them to control your behavior or your attitudes toward yourself, others, and God. Forgiveness is God's way of closing one season of our life and starting another.

- Unforgiveness exists when there are unanswered questions, discouragement, or disappointment that need to be dealt with. Unforgiveness can lead to bitterness, shame, and regret. These unresolved feelings keep you holding onto the pain in the hope that it will someday change the outcome of the situation. Also, unforgiveness allows us to think that somehow God has more to say about the experience, relationship, or person when usually he doesn't.

Forgiveness and unforgiveness applied to the same situation can change how you see your purpose in life, your destiny in God, and your value to others. Unforgiveness leads to brokenness and strangleholds; forgiveness allows healing, mends the broken places, and activates God's plan of grace for our lives. We now have grace that we share with others and allow them to experience the same freedom. The "new" thing from Isaiah 43:19 is the freedom that comes in emotional healing and God's grace. The "new" things are the different people, relationships, and experiences that you can enjoy with the new perspective of the power of God's grace.

How Do You Forgive and Break Strongholds?

Meditate on the following Scripture passages. Also, ask God to give you the grace and opportunity to seek his forgiveness for yourself and others.

- *Confess your trespasses to one another, and pray for one another that you may be healed.* James 5:16

- *If we confess our sins, He is faithful and just to forgive us our sins . . .* 1 John 1:9

- *Therefore, as the elect of God, holy and beloved, put on tender mercies, kindness, humility, meekness, longsuffering; bearing with one another and forgiving one another, if anyone has a complaint against another; even as Christ forgave you, so you also must do.* Colossians 3:12

- *"For this commandment which I command you today is not too mysterious for you, nor is it far off.* Deuteronomy 30:11

The Reverend Clay Evans released a song a few years ago called "Reach beyond the Break." It was one of my favorite songs to play when I was a gospel music announcer. It tells a compelling story of a boy who is caught in a storm and struggles to survive after his rope, his lifeline to safety, breaks. As he panics, he calls out for help and hears the instructions "Reach beyond the break." Initially, he hesitates, but eventually does so and is brought to safety.

> ✻ RECOVERY TIP:
> *Relationships are not easy—there are cycles of intimacy and distancing. It is natural that you find recovering from a relationship one thing and hope in a future relationship quite another.*

What I like about the story is the fact that the boy was so focused on the break in the rope that he didn't realize that there was another piece, beyond the break, that could lead to safety. As Christians, we must also realize that there is a "peace" beyond our heartbreaks and emotional disappointments. The peace, no matter how fragile, can lead us to safety if we grab onto it.

When you decide to transition back into socializing and dating, keep in mind that there is peace beyond your heartbreak, and it is within your reach. Sometimes your pain may seem so great that peace seems unattainable, but you have to rely on your faith. It's there because in God's presence there is peace and God is present with us, especially during our storms. I have to keep this in mind as I reenter the dating world. (I haven't kissed dating goodbye—I plan to enjoy the friendships I can develop from healthy and mature dating relationships.)

I have talked to many others who assure me that I'm not alone in my uncertainty about peace being within my reach. You can be so focused on the heartbreak caused by "Darrell" or "Diana" that you can't see beyond it. It's especially hard when others with their "ends justify the means" mentality and actions seem to get what you want and wish for.

If you're brokenhearted, you may have mastered the art of recovery and of getting over "it." For whatever reason, however, you may be unable to hold on to the promises and hope of the future. If you find it easy to get over someone that hurts you, but are not able to grasp the peace, you have the potential to begin a frustrating cycle of reaching and releasing, of emotional distancing and intimacy. In relationships it's like a confusing dance of go away, come closer.

This bizarre dance causes many to be unhappy while looking for another relationship to bring them happiness. And they are bitter when they realize that the relationship they thought they couldn't live without is slowly, emotionally, and spiritually dying.

> *God did this so that men would seek him*
> *and perhaps reach out for him and find him,*
> *though he is not far from each one of us.* Acts 17:27 NIV

I encourage you to set your focus "beyond the break" and grab on to the lifeline of peace that leads to emotional stability. God sent his Son Jesus Christ to breach the break that was caused by man's sin. He reached beyond that "break" and held on in an effort to reconcile us to him.

We must also reach beyond the emotional distance and detachment caused by heartbreak and emotional disappointment if we are to enjoy healthy romantic and platonic relationships.

> *Let all bitterness, wrath, anger, clamor and evil-speaking*
> *be put away from you, with all malice. And be kind*
> *to one another, tenderhearted, forgiving one another,*
> *even as God in Christ forgave you.* Ephesians 4:31–32

Many times I've bought grapes that looked juicy, fresh, and sun-ripened, but after tasting them I realized that I'd been "hood-winked" into buying some pretty-looking but bad-tasting, immature fruit. On the outside they looked good, but on the inside they still needed to mature. During my love hangover I felt the same disappointment when I realized that I looked "okay" on the outside, but I still needed to stay on the vine and mature, let go of some more of the pain, and grow on the inside. In other words, I needed to let God continue to work on healing my heart.

Our emotional maturity is like the growth process of grapes. If taken too soon from our "emotional" vines, we may seem okay, but not be as sweet as if we'd stayed on the vine and matured some more. More than likely, though, if we pridefully attempt to rush through the emotional upheaval after the loss of a relationship, we end up bitter and not as "sweet" and mature as if we'd grown with the "Son" through prayer, reading God's word, and building safe relationships with safe people.

I sometimes still struggle with answering the "Am I bitter or better because of what happened?" Honestly, there was a time when I allowed my disappointment to overshadow my desire to be healthy. Because I was embarrassed, I was distracted and over-whelmed by the loss. It sounds simple, but I almost missed the fact that my disappointment was to be acknowledged and not repressed.

> *Finally, brethren, whatever things are true, whatever things*
> *are noble, whatever things are just, whatever things are pure,*
> *whatever things are lovely, whatever things are of good report,*
> *if there is any virtue and if there is anything praiseworthy—*
> *meditate on these things.* Philippians 4:8

Being the child of a career military man, I've experienced the joys and confusion of moving. It was always fun looking forward to going somewhere new and seeing things I'd never seen before. It was also an uneasy time because of the thought of being someplace new and seeing things I'd never seen before. My parents used to reassure us that it was our attitude about the move that would determine whether the move would become something good or something bad. Imagine my surprise as an elementary school child when I began to look forward to the usual dreaded move and I started to think about the good, and not bad, parts of the move.

> **RECOVERY TIP:**
> *If you are suffering from a love hangover and having trouble moving beyond the pain, don't hesitate to pray and meditate on Scripture to help find your purpose.*

This example from my past brings me to answer how to move from emotional devastation to emotional wholeness. You have to think about positive things and what is going well in your life. This may be hard to do if you're crying over a lost love, but it can be done. I remember when I was still in shock over the breakup and would have crying fits for no apparent reason. I got to the point where I wanted to move beyond those fits and would recite Philippians 4:9. Sometimes it didn't seem like it would change my mood, but I eventually noticed a shift in my attitude and, ultimately, my thoughts. I used to have to force myself to think of good, honest, pure, things.

> *To everything there is a season,*
> *a time for every purpose under heaven.* Ecclesiastes 3:1

Once you discover your purpose, you will also discover that there is inevitable pain to your purpose, not a physical pain that weakens your body, but an emotional and spiritual pain that burdens you down.

Using weights during exercise helps strengthen the muscles and increases the quality of the workout. I had to learn how to use the weight of my purpose to strengthen me. It was painful and uncomfortable. But I know that, because I am being obedient to what God has called me to do for this season of my life, blessings and favor will be added to my life.

When I first accepted my purpose as a writer and a speaker, I was puzzled about why I sometimes felt anxious and unsure. I had prayed and knew that I was doing God's will, but I still felt just plain weird. Part of this pain was rooted in the conflict between God's will and my plans for my life.

When I started *The Dallas Weekly* column in October 2000, I wasn't planning to expose myself or the most intimate details of my life. I struggled with God over just how much information about my past relationship(s) that I would divulge. I didn't want the thousands of readers of *The Dallas Weekly* to know that I had been dumped by my last boyfriend. I actually tried to reason with God that most of the readers wouldn't actually care. The mother of all writers' blocks prevented me from writing even one paragraph during this time.

It wasn't until I said (and sincerely meant) that I was going to write what God told me to write that the words and paragraphs and ideas began to flow.

The strength came from an increase in my prayer life. I prayed every day for God to take away the burden; now I use the same time to pray that he will receive the glory from what I write. But the point is, I began to pray on a consistent basis. I've also become more confident in my relationship with God, in knowing that he was with me. The pain was for a season, but the blessings of being obedient to God's purpose for my life, will last my lifetime.

Post-Love Hangover Reflection

BITTER OR BETTER—MORE THAN LIKELY, your love hangover experience will leave you in one of these two categories. Bitter because what you wanted to happen didn't, or better because you realize that what you wanted really wasn't God's best for you. How you will deal with disappointment is one of the most important decisions that you'll have to make when faced with the loss of a relationship. Why? Because how effectively you deal with disappointment affects how much or how little you will trust intimately in the future. Your desire to remain safe and pain-free will convince you that the best way to avoid disappointment is to avoid trusting yourself and others.

Well-meaning family and friends may even try to persuade you to not deal with the disappointment of a broken heart because it is a sign that you are bitter and foolishly holding onto the past. You'll find out that not properly accepting and dealing with this disappointment will cause bitterness. You have to learn to resist allowing others to define who you are and how you should feel about the loss of your relationship.

The sadness I sometimes feel is now for the loss of what could have been—and the reality that the relationship was not healthy because my ex and I were not healthy. It took maturity and the passage of time to offer up my disappointment to God, to turn a sour experience into one that could be offered up as *"an offering . . . a sweet aroma to the Lord"* (Numbers 15:14).

Whispers of Love

Pause for Reflection

It's In the Valleys I Grow

Sometimes life seems hard to bear,
Full of sorrow, trouble and woe,
It's then I have to remember,
That it's in the valleys I grow.

If I always stayed on the mountaintop
And never experienced pain,
I would never appreciate God's love
And would be living in vain.

I have so much to learn
And my growth is very slow.
Sometimes I need the mountaintops,
But it's in the valleys I grow.

I do not always understand
Why things happen as they do,
But I am very sure of one thing,
My Lord will see me through.

My little valleys are nothing
When I picture Christ on the cross.
He went through the valley of death;
His victory was Satan's loss.

Forgive me, Lord, for complaining
When I'm feeling so very low.
Just give me a gentle reminder
That it's in the valleys I grow.

Continue to strengthen me, Lord,
And use my life each day,
To share your love with others
And help them find their way.

Thank you for valleys, Lord,
For this one thing I know
The mountaintops are glorious,
But it's in the valleys I grow!

© 2001 Tracy Mayfield

Describe how you understand God's purpose in allowing you to experience the pain of your broken relationship.

Yea, though I walk through the valley of the shadow of death,
I will fear no evil; For You are with me;
Your rod and Your staff, they comfort me.

Psalm 23:4

Telling others about what you've overcome is an important part
of healing. What would you tell others was the purpose behind
your emotional pain?

> *The LORD builds up Jerusalem;*
> *He gathers together the outcasts of Israel.*
> *He heals the brokenhearted And binds up their wounds.*
> Psalm 147:2–3

Loneliness, frustration, anger, and anxiety are a few emotions that
are your traveling companions when you walk through your
valley. What emotions do you feel could be your companions on
the mountaintop?

> *For godly sorrow produces repentance leading to salvation,*
> *not to be regretted; but the sorrow of the world produces death.*
> 2 Corinthians 7:10

What has this experience taught you about God? How did it
change your relationship with him?

> *Multitudes, multitudes in the valley of decision!*
> *For the day of the LORD is near in the valley of decision.*
> Joel 3:14

What effective tools for survival did you use in your valley experience? (These could be prayer, fasting, etc.)

Appendix A

When All Else Fails . . . See the Doctor

*"The breakup of an important relationship is the most
traumatic of human experiences. In many ways we can more
easily cope with the death of a loved one. Although we don't
understand death, at least we understand its finality."*

—Dr. Cherry Lee, *Surviving the Breakup of a Relationship*

EXPERTS SUGGEST that the healing period of a breakup may last anywhere between one and three years! Quite some time: long enough to earn a law degree! After all the tears, denial, bargaining, contemplating, reminiscing, finger-pointing, or self-blaming comes the acceptance. The recovery process and self-healing strategies differ from person to person. Some prefer a spiritual approach while others may follow the advice of a variety of books, columns, articles, or reputable psychotherapists, like Oprah's favorite, Phil McGraw. Regardless of the ingredients in the recipe, the desired product remains the same—inner peace, resolution, and the courage to love again.

Oftentimes while climbing and attempting to conquer our personal Mt. Everest en route to recovery, we fail to recognize the need and benefit of seeking professional help. We become so focused on the everyday, step-by-step, taking it "one day at a time" approach, not realizing the journey can often be shorter and the mountain climb less steep and treacherous with a little mental health assistance. This is usually either because of denial or simply out of ignorance, not knowing that quality and affordable counseling actually exists.

Of course, now you may think, "In the middle of all these tear-filled, sleepless nights and self-pity parties, the last thing I need is to add a 'shrink' or a therapist to my not-so-proud-to-admit list!"

> RECOVERY TIP:
> *There is no measuring tape to pain. Prolonged symptoms of depression or feeling down may indicate the need for professional help.*

Many people who visit a therapist initially felt the very same way and believed it would all pass with time and tears. Society perceives needing help from a total stranger in dealing with our emotional turmoil as a sign of weakness. This misconception is unfair and senseless, and it can inhibit the self-healing process.

So you ask, "When or how will I know that I need to see a therapist?" The answer lies in how significantly and how long the "mourning after" impairs other areas of your everyday life—primarily socially and occupationally. Unfortunately, there is no measuring tape for us to conveniently use to predict how long the pain should remain after a breakup. Of course, one would naturally assume that the mourning after a divorce of a ten-year marriage with three children would last longer than the mourning after a ten-month relationship with no kids involved.

Various factors play a role: the presence (or absence) of an emotional support system; spirituality and spiritual wellness; how soon after the actual breakup you *begin* accepting that it *could be* over; being socially isolated and withdrawn; having reasons to "fuel" the initial animosity that unfortunately often results (infidelity, emotional or physical abuse, poor parenting, etc.); and how deep your love was for your mate at the time of the separation, just to name a few.

The terms "sad," "depressed," "feeling blue," and "down in the dumps" are all commonly used to describe how we feel during this emotionally fragile time. People often present to their therapist or psychiatrist using these words. They all describe the mood of the individual. The diagnosis of clinical depression, requiring professional mental health therapy and/or medication, results after two weeks of four or more of the following symptoms:

- Sleep disturbance—a pattern of increased or decreased hours of sleep or quality of sleep (frequent awakenings) compared to what was normal before the sadness.
- Interest—a decreased interest in things that we used to derive pleasure from (sports, reading, recreational activities, etc.).
- Guilt—a sense of guilt, often self-blame, surrounding the reasons the relationship failed.
- Energy—decreased energy, often feeling tired, not well rested
- Concentration—problems with concentration and short-term memory.
- Appetite—increased or decreased appetite; undesirable weight gain or weight loss, often leading to significant distress
- Psychomotor agitation—irritability, anxiety, and/or inability to remain still; restlessness.
- Suicidal—thoughts or ideas of desiring death or self-harm, sense of hopelessness, feeling that death is better than having to continue enduring the hurt and pain.

If you have experienced feelings of sadness and four or more of these symptoms for at least two weeks, if you're at the point where your job performance (level of stress tolerance, ability to perform duties, decreased quality of performance) and social life (relationships, friends, family, and associates) have both noticeably suffered impairment, you may very well be experiencing clinical depression, and you may benefit from psychotherapy and/or medication.

If you have less than four of these symptoms and/or your symptoms have not lasted two weeks, you may be on your way to clinical depression.

This clinical information and criteria for self-diagnosis is by no means intended to be a substitution for a professional mental health evaluation. It is merely to introduce you to and make you aware of some of the signs and symptoms of clinical depression. Don't hesitate to seek professional mental health care.

Coping Mechanisms

DEALING WITH A LOVE HANGOVER is very trying, tedious, and devastating. In the process of accepting the ordeal, we tend to use various defense mechanisms. The primary purpose of these mechanisms is to ease the anxiety, frustration, and emotional turmoil that are experienced during the recovery process. Psychoanalyst/theorist Sigmund Freud developed the theory of ego psychology, composed of the id, ego, and superego. Under this theory, the id represented the drives and "basic instincts" of the mind. The superego contained the sense of right and wrong, most commonly learned from parental and societal influences. The ego was responsible for environmental adaptation and for the resolution of conflict. In the case of dealing with a love hangover, of the three, the ego remains very busy! Following are scenarios for and explanations of coping mechanisms.

Denial—failure to acknowledge a disturbing aspect of external reality.

And you shall know the truth,
and the truth shall make you free. John 8:32

"Lawrence and I have three wonderful children and twenty-seven years of marriage to cherish. After ten years of pure suspicion and then eventually catching him in the act, I grew to accepting and dealing with his infidelity. I was a good wife, helping to build his business from the first mailed sheet of stationery. I never knew a three-story, seven-bedroom, four-bathroom dream home would leave me feeling so unhappy and empty inside. The kids all grown and married and living in different cities makes it all the more difficult. Seven months, one week, four days, and counting . . . he'll come back to me. His new wife isn't even prettier than me. He promised it was forever."

Denial is when we fail to acknowledge and accept a disturbing aspect of our external reality. For example, the wife in this statement is clearly in denial that the relationship is no longer viable.

Rationalization—distortion of reality that makes an undesirable act or event seem more desirable.

> *Woe to those who call evil good, and good evil;*
> *Who put darkness for light, and light for darkness;*
> *Who put bitter for sweet, and sweet for bitter.* Isaiah 5:20

"I understand why she left me for her boss. He was CEO of the corporation, a much better provider of her needs and wants. She had to be kidding with all that talk about our boring sex life."

Rationalization usually occurs when it's easier to accept a perverted version of the truth because it's easier to handle. Because the pain of the truth is so debilitating, this coping mechanism makes the truth more desirable and acceptable.

Reaction Formation—an unacceptable thought or feeling that is transformed into its opposite.

For we dare not class ourselves or compare ourselves
with those who commend themselves.
But they, measuring themselves by themselves,
and comparing themselves among themselves, are not wise.
2 Corinthians 10:12

"When I talk about how Anthony left me for my best friend, Charlene, I can't help but laugh! I mean, those two are not your typical match made in heaven. She has the class and sophistication of a dishrag and the sex appeal of a porcupine. What in the world was Tony thinking! To leave the four wonderful years we shared, a highly anticipated engagement party with some of the most affluent people and even a few celebrities invited, and a Bellaire condominium, is just insane. In fact, it's downright hilarious!

Reaction formation occurs when our pride and shame from our emotional hurt allow us to make a feeling, thought, or attitude the opposite of what it truly is. In this example, laughter replaces the obvious anger that this person is feeling.

Repression—aspects of reality, like memories and impulses, that are completely separated from conscious awareness.

So then, my beloved brethren,
let every man be swift to hear, slow to speak, slow to wrath;
for the wrath of man does not produce the righteousness of God.
James 1:19–20

"Wallace, have you seen Jonathan lately? He has been on a rampage!"

"No, I haven't. Fill me in."

"Last Monday, on a clear-skies, sunny day, he crashed his Jaguar into a light post, no other cars involved. Wednesday he smashed a beer bottle over some guy's head at the bar for smiling in his direction, only to find the guy was flirting with a woman sitting next to him. He spent Friday night in jail after smarting off to a cop who pulled him over for a taillight that was out . . ."

"You must be kidding. Yeah, right. Jonathan, the perfect gentleman?"

"He actually shoved the cop and called him a fat pig-in-a-donut! I tell you, man, he has not been the same since Courtney dumped him two weeks ago."

Oftentimes, the repressed anger and rage left by unanswered questions will force us to physically act out our displeasure and discomfort.

Splitting—occurs when an individual psychologically separates positive qualities into one individual or group and negative qualities into another.

> *Therefore, you are inexcusable, O man,*
> *whoever you are who judge, for in whatever you judge another*
> *you condemn yourself; for you who judge practice the same things.*
> *But we know that the judgment of God is according to truth*
> *against those who practice such things.* Romans 2:1–2

"Stephanie is the third and final ambitious, independent woman I will ever date! First it was Lisa: She wouldn't even let me open a door for her or advise her on what stock options to buy. For God's sake, I have only been in investment banking for fourteen years! Then there was Erica. She was so competitive, it was annoying! From salaries, to time between job promotions, to even percentage of body fat! Stephanie was a combination of the two, plus a unique and mesmerizing charm and sense of presence. With each woman, I always felt inadequate and insecure. I was always straining my brain and pocketbook trying to keep them pleased and satisfied. Whether it was intentional or not, dating them became intimidating. Never again! The last girl I dated that didn't make me feel this way was Alexis, my high school sweetheart. That was over twenty-two years ago, but my memories are fond and full of bliss. She was dependent, submissive, and naive. Of course, I never took advantage of her naivete, but it made me feel secure knowing she was not exposed to many worldly mentalities and tendencies of other people. If she didn't realize how common cheating was, she wouldn't dare think about it! No worries. No lies. No flimsy alibis. No fears of losing her to some other guy! Yeah, that's the ticket: submissive women only. A woman should always need a man for almost everything! There is no other option. Never again will I entertain the thought of dating the independent, self-sufficient type!"

This coping mechanism lets us split all negative and positive traits into separate categories. This separation is normally caused by the inability to tolerate the ambivalence we feel after the end of the relationship.

Projection—attribution of uncomfortable internal feelings or thoughts, especially anger or guilt, to other individuals.

> *"Hypocrite! First remove the plank from your own eye,*
> *and then you will see clearly to remove the speck*
> *from your brother's eye."* Matthew 7:5

"Jason, did I not tell you to call me as soon as you made it to Rachel's house and call me when you were leaving? I get so frustrated when you say one thing and do another. You promised me you would always let me know you were okay. Son, I know you are eighteen now and practically a grown man, but I just want to know that you are safe!"

"Mom, I did call. I tried four or five times, but the line was busy . . ."

"I don't want to hear anymore, young man. You are grounded from seeing Rachel for two weeks! Now go to your room."

"That's fine. Rachel and I broke up anyway. She has issues. Mom, where's Dad? He hasn't been home in two days."

Projection is when we are angry at ourselves, but then turn that anger on others. It is easier to accuse others and focus on their "mess" than deal with our own issues.

Dissociation—sealing of disturbing thoughts or emotions from consciousness.

> *Only take heed to yourself, and diligently keep yourself,*
> *lest you forget the things your eyes have seen*
> *and lest they depart from your heart all the days of your life.*
> Deuteronomy 4:9

"Nicole, what are you doing? Are you roasting marshmallows over the fireplace?"

"Yes, I had a sudden craving for some roasted marshmallows! Want some?"

"The doctor told you to stay in bed to rest your bruised shoulder and neck. Where is your arm sling? Nicole, are you insane? Your arm is broken in three places! I know you are in a hurry to get over Corey and him abusing you and leaving you but . . ."

"Kara, did I ever tell you how much I love the smell of roasting marshmallows and sitting by the fireplace? There's nothing much better on a cold winter night like this."

"Oh, my God! Is that your and Corey's wedding album in the fireplace? What happened to all your pictures on the wall?"

"You know, Kara, photo albums and cheap wood picture frames make pretty good firewood."

With dissociation the pain of our memories is more influential than the reality and truth of our present. We seal off uncomfortable and unmanageable thoughts and deal with them at a distance.

Fantasy—substitution of reality with a less disturbing view of the world.

> *He who tills his land will have plenty of bread,*
> *but he who follows frivolity will have poverty enough!*
>
> Proverbs 28:19

"Angelina, why are you still serving me breakfast in bed and wearing skimpy negligees to bed? It's been three months now. The divorce has been finalized. We promised we would remain civil and stay under the same roof until Kevin and Kyla graduated. We only have two months to go. Then you can have the house and I'll go live with Donna. Let's not make this complicated."

"Sweetheart, would you like your eggs softly scrambled or sunnyside up? Besides, Donna is no good for you. She's a freelance photographer. She has no 401(k) and no job security whatsoever. No man in his right mind would leave this for something so worthless. Orange juice or coffee, honey?"

"Did you hear anything I just said?"

"No, but I'll bring both coffee and orange juice and sunnyside up for you, young man. Gotta watch that cholesterol! I plan to keep that heart of yours ticking for a long time and a lotta loving."

Fantasy means actively seeking to make real what is not real. The substitution allows us to deal with a less disturbing view of reality.

Appendix B

 Recommended Web Sites

Surviving the Breakup of a Relationship
http://www.cybercollege.com/sing11.htm

Relationship Self-Help Programs for Couples, Singles, and Those
in Transition
http://drmichaelbroder.com/relationship.htm

Letting Go of Your Ended Love Relationship: Overcoming the
Pain of a Breakup or Divorce in the Shortest Possible Period
of Time ★ (Michael Broder, Ph.D.)
http://drmichaelbroder.com/relationship.htm

Mars and Venus Starting Over: A Practical Guide for Finding
Love After a Painful Breakup, Divorce, or Loss of a Loved
One ★ (Michael Gray, Ph.D.)
http://consciousmedia.com/consciousmedia/0061098388

Lovingyou.com: Dating: Breakup
http://lovingyou.com/dating/breakup/breakup.shtml

Loss of a Relationship: Divorce, Breaking up, Estranged Parent—
Psychological Self-Help
http://mentalhelp.net/psyhelp/

A Family Breakup Affects Us All
http://www.childfun.com/parents/d.shtml

Mental Health Net
http://mentalhelp.net

Recommended Books

Anderson, Don. *Drawing Closer, Growing Stronger (Road Toward Consistency: How to Guarantee Your Life Will Really Count).* Sisters, Oregon: Multnomah Publishers, 1997.

Arterburn, Stephen; Felton, Jack. *More Jesus, Less Religion: Moving from Rules to Relationship.* Colorado Springs, Colorado: Waterbrook Press, 2000.

Arterburn, Stephen; Neal, Connie. *The Emotional Freedom Workbook: Take Control of Your Life and Experience Emotional Healing.* Nashville, Tennessee: Thomas Nelson, 1995.

Arterburn, Stephen; Rinck, Dr. Meg J. *Avoiding Mr. Wrong: And What to Do if You Didn't.* Nashville, Tennessee: Thomas Nelson, 2000.

Arterburn, Stephen; Stoop, David. *Seven Keys to Spiritual Renewal Workbook.* Wheaton, Illinois: Tyndale House Publishers, 1998.

Gillooly, Sheila. *Venus in Spurs.* New York: Henry Holt and Company, 1997.

Hemfelt, Robert; Minirth, Frank; Meier, Paul. *Love Is a Choice: Recovery for Codependent Relationships.* Nashville, Tennessee: Thomas Nelson, 1996.

Hendrix, Harville. *Getting the Love You Want: A Guide for Couples.* New York: Henry Holt and Company, 2001.

Lucado, Max. *In the Grip of Grace: You Can't Fall Beyond His Love.* Nashville, Tennessee: Word Publishing, 1996.

Mains, David R. *Healing the Dysfunctional Church Family.* Destiny Image, 1995.

Rose, Ron. *Diary of God: Stories of God's Incredible Encounters with His People.* Sisters, Oregon: Multnomah Publishers, 1997.

Rupp, Joyce. *The Cup of Our Life*. Notre Dame, Indiana: Ave Maria Press, 1997.

Smith, Manuel J. *When I Say No, I Feel Guilty*. New York: Bantam, 1975.

Sproul, R.C. *The Invisible Hand: Do All Things Really Work for Good?* Nashville, Tennessee: Word Publishing, 1996.

Touchpoints: God's Answers for Your Daily Needs. Wheaton, Illinois: Tyndale House, 1996.

Turner, Kevin Lane. *Journey to the Other Side of Life: Understanding Your Emotions*. Ashley Down Publishing Co, 1995.

Westberg, Granger E. *Good Grief: A Constructive Approach to the Problem of Loss*. Fortress Press, 1986.

Williams, Leslie. *Seduction of the Lesser Gods*. Nashville, Tennessee: Word Publishing, 1998.

Scripture Index

Old Testament

Genesis   18:14   *169*

Numbers   15:14   *200*

Deuteronomy   4:9   *213*
    30:11   *196*

Joshua   1:9   *48, 148*

1 Chronicles   16:34   *170*

Nehemiah   8:10   *138, 147*

Psalm   4:8   *139*
    5:3   *49*
    7:21, 26   *153*
    23:4   *202*
    34:8   *73*
    55:21   *163*
    59:16   *22, 75*
    71:5   *170*
    91   *65*
    92:2   *171*
    119:40   *148*
    126:5   *48*
    126:5–6   *176*
    143:8   *17*
    147:2–3   *203*

Proverbs   2:10   *50*
    3:24   *106*
    3:5–6   *182*
    9:6   *108*
    10:12   *170*
    15:4   *159*
    16:18–19   *182*
    19:11   *72*
    27:6   *154*
    27:6   *73*
    27:9   *61*
    28:19   *216*
    30:5   *137*

Ecclesiastes   3:1   *198*

Isaiah   5:20   *209*
    12:2   *181*
    26:3   *148*
    43:19   *192*
    58:11   *176*

Lamentations   3:22–23   *21, 107*
    3:25   *148*

Daniel   1:8–20   *67–68*

Joel   3:14   *203*

Jonah   1:3   *161*

Zechariah   13:6   *62*

New Testament

Matthew	7:5	212
	12:43–45	146
Mark	10:52	179
John	4:15	166
	8:32	208
	10:10	141
	15:15	61
Acts of the Apostles	17:27	196
Romans	5:1	180
	12:18	174
1 Corinthians	10:13	148
2 Corinthians	7:10	203
	10:12	210
Galatians	5:1	148
	5:22	146
	6:7	105
Ephesians	4:31–32	196
	4:32	106, 148

Philippians	4:6–7	73
	4:7	68
	4:8	57, 199
	4:13	76
Colossians	3:12	194
2 Thessalonians	3:3	148
2 Timothy	1:7	48
	3:2–4	152
	3:5	156
Titus	1:16	155
Hebrews	13:15	106
James	1:16–17	159
	1:19–20	47, 210
	3:13	148
	5:16	194
2 Peter	2:19	164
1 John	1:9	194
	4:4	18
	4:7–8	147

Shewanda Riley, M.A., is a Dallas-based media professional and is currently the news director and morning show producer for KNON Radio. She is also the Dallas correspondent for the Sheridan Broadcasting Network. Ms. Riley has worked as a producer and on-air talent for radio stations (KOAI, KRBV, KHNV, KWRD) in Dallas, and (KCHL, KCJZ) in San Antonio, and for Armed Forces Network (Fuerth, Germany). She was a professional fellow at the 2000 National Association of Broadcasters Executive Development Program for Radio Broadcasters. She has been featured discussing relationships on ABC's national radio broadcast *The Touch* and on the national TV broadcast *The Potter's Touch*, hosted by T.D. Jakes.

One of Riley's most recent achievements as a writer includes being a contributor for *The Women of Color Study Bible* (Tyndale House/Nia Publishing). She writes relationship columns for *The Dallas Weekly* and *Keep It Real,* a singles magazine in England. An avid reader, Riley has also edited a number of books. She is an adjunct professor of English at Tarrant County Community College–Northeast Campus in Hurst, Texas.

Ms. Riley graduated from St. Mary's University with a B.A. in English-Communication Arts, and from Southern Methodist University with an M.A. in English. She serves on the board of the Skillful Living Center and is Jobs and Internships Committee Chairperson for the DFW Association of Black Communicators.

Special thanks to Craig McKenney and Yokima Cureton for their editorial expertise. And much love to Monique McDaniel, Tracy Mayfield, Dormel Cobbs-Thompson, Wayne Tillman, Karen Gaines, and Anja Blackadar for their creative contributions.

Special thanks also to so many people who have opened their hearts to me over the years. First, much love to my family: Frank and Nealie Riley, Mia Morris, Alma Matthews, Natasha Merrill, Vina Mae Alexander, Alex, Alicia, Ashley, Dominique, Jennifer, Robert, Jr.

Thanks to my friends: Charnae Williams, LyFranshua Pipkins, Vanessa Weatherspoon, Wayne Tillman, Monique McDaniel, Ruth Mayfield, Thomas Mitchem, Chris Gilliam, Patricia Harris, Ariel Chriss, Cedric Varner.

To those who provided spiritual comfort and guidance: Rev. Paul Royal, Pastor Janet Bell-Odom, Rev. Jerry Christian, Chaplain Bridget Goines, Rev. Karen Gaines, Rev. Toni Hatchett, Pastors David and Claudette Copeland, Bishop T.D. Jakes, David and Keely Collier, Revs. Eric and Jacci Copeland, Elder Carolyn Gilbert, and Pastor Keith Shuler.

(If I have failed to list your name, please count it to my head and not my heart!)

And I would especially like to mention those whose deliberate and inadvertent actions caused me pain and heartache. It's been said that we should thank our enemies and those who hurt us because they put us on our knees and closer to God. To those who put me on my knees, I say, God Bless You!

—Shewanda Riley

Dr. Germaine B. Hawkins, D.O., a native of Houston, earned his Bachelor of Science degree in Biomedical Science from Texas A&M University and then earned his Doctorate of Osteopathic Medicine at the University of North Texas Health Science Center. Dr. Hawkins is currently a psychiatry resident at John Peter Smith Hospital in Fort Worth, Texas. Gifted with a picturesque and thought-provoking writing style, his work can be found in the "Love Hangover" column in *The Dallas Weekly* and in various medical journals.

Dr. Hawkins' contribution to the book is a clinical viewpoint based on his experiences working with patients. He often reminds patients that the commitment to love someone is and will always remain a "choice, one that can be recanted, reconsidered, and even reversed." Dr. Hawkins hopes to remove the negative stigma associated with seeking professional mental health. He believes that society remains overly critical to those who "just can't cope," which unfortunately discourages many from receiving much-needed counseling.

Dr. Hawkins is actively involved in the community and in various organizations, including the National Medical Association, American Psychiatric Association, and Kappa Alpha Psi Fraternity Incorporated.

Special thanks, first and foremost: I must give honor to the One who has made it all possible, my Lord and Savior, Jesus Christ.

Dad, I hold fond memories of you. You were a God-fearing man, the epitome of an Angel. Your unconditional love and support I will always treasure; like a precious jewel I will keep you locked in the depths of my heart and soul. The morals, self-confidence, and Christian ways you instilled in me are priceless. You played an essential role in the molding of the man I am today. You led by example not empty or short-lived promises. My only desire is that I may one day emulate your many admirable and altruistic ways.

To my mother, Mrs. Charlesetta Hawkins, I love you dearly. Thank you for the many sacrifices you have made over the years, supplying me with all my needs and most of my wants.

To my family, siblings and their spouses, Rita and (Cleveland) Robinson, Victor Moten, Debra Turner, Robert and (Regina) Hawkins, and Chandra Hawkins; Lonnie and Beatrice Hawkins and family, Dorothy and Christina Briggs, Cora Hobbs, Wade and Betty Johnson and family, Pastor and Mrs. Joe Russell, and the church family of Greater Jerusalem Baptist Church Houston, Texas, and my many aunts, uncles, nieces, and nephews.

Adria and Donna Carter, *On Pointe Productions,* the office of Ralph Brooks, M.D., Debbara Dixon, Monika Shah, D.O., Timothy Cowthorn, D.O., Marcus Denmon and family, Kelly and Tonya Yancy, Robert Carter, Ph. D., Alfred Hill, Maurice Williams, Ph.D., Vincent Allen, Christopher Hall, Clarence Estes, Kerry Brown, Michael Hendricks, Jeff Pollard, Andre Bradley, Ryan McKeown, Shelton Dotson III, and the Brothers of the Nu Alpha Chapter of Kappa Alpha Psi Fraternity, Texas A&M University.

To the many others I have failed to mention who have supported me over the years, I thank you sincerely.

—Germaine Hawkins